W9-DAD-560

THE NEW SENIOR MAN

THE NEW SENIOR MAN

Exploring New Horizons,
New Opportunities

Thelma Reese and Barbara M. Fleisher

ROWMAN & LITTLEFIELD
Lanham • Boulder • New York • London

Published by Rowman & Littlefield
A wholly owned subsidiary of The Rowman & Littlefield Publishing Group, Inc.
4501 Forbes Boulevard, Suite 200, Lanham, Maryland 20706
www.rowman.com

Unit A, Whitacre Mews, 26-34 Stannary Street, London SE11 4AB

Copyright © 2017 by Thelma Reese and Barbara M. Fleisher

All rights reserved. No part of this book may be reproduced in any form or by any electronic or mechanical means, including information storage and retrieval systems, without written permission from the publisher, except by a reviewer who may quote passages in a review.

British Library Cataloguing in Publication Information Available

Library of Congress Cataloging-in-Publication Data

Names: Reese, Thelma, 1933– author. | Fleisher, Barbara M., 1930–2016 author.
Title: The new senior man : exploring new horizons, new opportunities / Thelma Reese and Barbara M. Fleisher.
Description: Lanham : Rowman & Littlefield, [2017] | Includes bibliographical references.
Identifiers: LCCN 2017008262 (print) | LCCN 2017025091 (ebook) | ISBN 9781442271975 (electronic) | ISBN 9781442271968 (cloth : alk. paper)
Subjects: LCSH: Retirees. | Older men—Retirement. | Retirement—Psychological aspects.
Classification: LCC HQ1062 (ebook) | LCC HQ1062 .F5643 2017 (print) | DDC 305.26/1—dc23
LC record available at https://lccn.loc.gov/2017008262

♾ ™ The paper used in this publication meets the minimum requirements of American National Standard for Information Sciences Permanence of Paper for Printed Library Materials, ANSI/NISO Z39.48-1992.

Printed in the United States of America

Dedicated to men who shaped our lives by nurturing, supporting, protecting, and inspiring:

Isadore Fine, Benjamin Terdiman, Morton Fine, Marvin Terdiman, Daniel Fleisher, and Harvey Reese

CONTENTS

INTRODUCTION

"**W**hat are those ElderChicks[1] doing writing a book about men?" We realize that this question may be occurring to you as you open this book. We can explain.

A few years ago, we wrote a book called *The New Senior Woman: Reinventing the Years Beyond Mid-Life*.[2] Some of the women in your life may have read it or heard us talk about it. We wrote it when we realized that among our contemporaries we might find the role models we needed who could help us navigate a new world that our mothers and grandmothers never knew. Not only had our context, the world we live in, changed dramatically, but our lives were also being extended, quite literally. A woman retiring from work in her early sixties might look forward to another active third of her life. What could women who were living these years well tell the rest of us? Well, it turned out they had a lot to tell us—and they did. And what they told us and all the women who read our book turned out to be valuable in providing examples and inspiration for the longevity that was suddenly upon us.

Invariably, wherever we have talked about our book and the issues raised by the women we meet, someone in the audience asks, "What about men? Where's the book about men?" The questioner may be a man or woman, but someone *always* asks. After all, men are living longer, too. They have had to adjust to rapidly advancing technology and the challenges that come with longer life. When we wrote about women, we considered, of course, the enormous effects on women's lives of their changing roles in society. We called it "women's lib" in the early days.

Those changes have affected the lives of the men they live with and work with just as much as they have affected women's own lives.

Both genders fortunate enough to reach what may turn out to be more than a whole third of active life will encounter ageism, which appears to bypass only people running for president of the United States or repeating long terms in Congress. Even unconsciously we have absorbed attitudes that may come as a shock when the stereotypes begin to include us. Men may encounter the effects of ageism earlier than ever, especially in the workplace. How else to explain the fact that since the American Society for Aesthetic Plastic Surgery began collecting statistical data in 1997, there has been a nearly 300 percent increase in the number of procedures performed on men?[3] The last five years have seen a 43 percent increase for men overall, including neck lifts, eye lifts, jawline recontouring, and liposuction.

Suppositions, generalizations, and "common wisdom" about men are reflected in the titles we found when we began to explore the possibility of this book. Men, we had been told, were not likely to want to talk about themselves, except perhaps to provide biographical facts or work histories. They were more likely to tell *what* they did than *why*. Unlike women, who usually have a network of intimates with whom they share the facts and emotions of their lives, men's conversations with each other were more likely to be about sports, work, politics, money, or physical activity. Most of the books written for men bear this idea out. The great majority of such books for men advise them on financial planning, real estate investment, and learning about the stock market, even mixing a better martini. Some suggest hobbies or ways to improve athletic skills. We found none that illuminate how men from varied walks of life and backgrounds are navigating life in a postpatriarchal world, one where the role of authority figure isn't so clearly defined and the prospect of an age of "retirement" is likely to be much longer than expected.

Perhaps even more than the women we met, men, too, can appreciate the need to redefine and reinvent their lives beyond the world of work. A man's context, the world he lives in, has changed, and so must he. It bears little resemblance to the world that his father and grandfather knew when they were sent off to retirement with the proverbial gold watch and the gift of a new set of golf clubs. The "new senior man" will find that the best is yet to come. Discovering what that best will be for him is the new adventure. The place to start, we found, was with the men from all walks of life who shared their time, their stories, and their discoveries so generously and openheartedly with us. They have found this unexpected gift of time exciting and fulfilling in ways that were unexpected.

Their stories, in their own words, will inspire your own.

I

MANNING UP TO RETIREMENT

Retired is being twice tired, I've thought: First tired of working, then tired of not.

—Richard Armour

WHY "MANNING UP"?

Remember when you first heard "man up"? Was it directed to you or, perhaps, another boy on your team when he couldn't hit the ball or when bullying reduced him to tears? You or your friend carried that voice internally. It said, "Don't cry" to the little boy; "Don't let them see how you feel" to the adolescent; "Pull yourself together and don't be a wimp" to the adult. It still speaks, signaling "Time to face the music of aging and make the most of it" to the man facing a next stage in life.

The world we're living in today is not the one where you first knew what "manning up" meant, however. In that world, whether you are simply approaching your first retirement now or are well into your eighties and beyond, your role was defined and implicitly conveyed as protector and provider, the stronger of the sexes, the one with built-in authority. Being "the man of the house" meant something different when you were a boy. Girls weren't told to "woman up"; after all, boys were in training to provide for and protect them. How is that early conditioning resonating with life in today's world? Are boys still being conditioned to be sole providers? Are girls learning "home ec" in school to prepare for life as "the little woman" at home?

AND WHAT *IS* "RETIREMENT" ANYWAY?

The whole concept of retirement has changed and continues to do so. Retirement was a radical idea in 1881 when Otto von Bismarck presented the idea to the Prussian Reichstag: government-run financial support for older members of society. Until then, people didn't retire; they worked until they died. There had been military pensions—scarcely enough to live on, however—but by the early 1890s the German government had created a retirement system that provided for citizens over the age of seventy, which was definitely beyond longevity expectations in those days. In the United States public pensions started in the mid-nineteenth century with mostly big-city employees such as police, firefighters, and teachers, followed by the American Express Company. By the 1920s, workers in a variety of industries were promised support for their later years, mostly based on retirement at age sixty-five. By the time the Social Security Act was passed in 1935, the official retirement age was sixty-five; *life expectancy for men was around fifty-eight.* By 1960, life expectancy was almost seventy, but people were now living past the age of sixty-five when they felt they were expected to work, and a new norm of spending decades at leisure became an expectation. Now, beginning in one's late fifties, such leisure looms unexpectedly long and boring without meaningful participation in life. Depending on when you start to think about retirement, you may have another half, third, quarter, or year to live well!

We use the term *retirement* in the conventional sense: you've left the work you've been doing for years and are about to embark on one of life's great changes. Or you're thinking about it. Perhaps you are only in your fifties and wisely planning ahead. Maybe you've been through several careers and need to reengage, or even fully engage for the first time. This change may be something you have chosen, or it may be the unwanted and unimagined change thrust upon you by a more "fluid" economy, or by age discrimination. Maybe living seems to be marked by a series of events that just help pass the time rather than use or further develop talents you've suspected or known you have. Is this an age or a stage? Is it just another phase? Everyone you meet in this book has shared the experience. We have something to learn from all of them.

NAME, RANK, AND SERIAL NUMBER!

Just who *are* you? For so many men, retirement can equal Identity Crisis. Sometimes leaving longtime work is like leaving a cocoon, and the emerging body feels strangely new and vulnerable. We found that for men more than women, identity is often tied so firmly to what one *did* that who one *is* got lost. As these men's lives will show, healthy, satisfying retirement can lead to finding answers to *who* and even *why* you are. Some do it by continuing, expanding, or further developing what they've always done—like musicians riffing on the music they've already written. Others discover what appear to be totally new and utterly absorbing fields of interests—and oftentimes the origins of these "new" occupations turn out to be found in youthful dreams that went unfulfilled while the exigencies of life kept noses to the grindstone. Still another cadre of men who are transitioning from career to retirement finds satisfaction and inspiration in the whole exploration process. Through volunteering, trying new activities, learning new skills, or reviving old dreams, they are finding what they were missing all along: themselves.

SOMEHOW, ALONG THE WAY TO NOW, THE CULTURE CHANGED AND CONTINUES TO CHANGE

Just look at the younger men around you—your sons, your grandsons, their peers. Their active participation in childcare is sending a different message to their children than your generation received. It is surely sending a message to you as well: our world has changed and continues to spin at a dizzying rate. But no "Stop the world; I want to get off!" for you. You can stay on, or even spin with it and make the present and coming years better than you expected. Keeping up is the challenge; being part of what is now known as the "Longevity Revolution" is the bonus. There is, however, a challenge you may not have expected. Perhaps, like **Oliver Franklin**, in chapter 5, you're no longer surprised when a new young hire at the office immediately addresses you by your first name, or maybe it gives you a little jolt, a reminder that a blurring of age differences bears examination.

Remember those times when you rolled your eyes at something your dad or grandfather said? Are you still doing it occasionally when a contemporary or someone older than you annoys or exasperates as he gropes for a name or a memory? Have you noticed anyone eye rolling or simply beginning to glance away while *you*'re still speaking? Even as your cohort of contemporaries grows in size beyond the world's expectations, a truth begins to dawn: a stereotype still exists, and you may not only be marked by it but also be contributing to it yourself, to your own detriment. It's called *ageism*.

Yet another challenge that requires manning up.

FACING AGEISM

Among the billions of dollars spent by Americans every year on plastic surgery, can you guess which group is rising fastest among those who elect to have it? That's right—men! Do you think age discrimination might have something to do with that?

The Age Discrimination in Employment Act of 1967 and its amendments prohibit employment discrimination based on age—from age forty and older—and many states provide additional protections for older workers, but try to prove that in Silicon Valley, where requests for nips and tucks by men in their early thirties (and younger!) are being reported by plastic surgeons. The high-tech world, pioneered by young men (desperately seeking women for their boardrooms, still stinging from charges of sexism), is populated largely by their mirror images. But while most men don't work in Silicon Valley or Silicon Alley, our world of celebrity consciousness and starshine reflects back everywhere we look. You don't have to live and work in those rarefied atmospheres to be affected by what goes on there. The whole world has a sense of awe at what the very young are accomplishing. The changes they make are transmitted to the world instantaneously through news and social media and most vividly through our own adaptations to them. Still using a rotary phone? Still have a landline? Give up your car yet? Is Skyping easing the strain of distance and physical separation in the family? Fill in your own blanks. And face it—each new thing carries with it the aura of youthful invention and inventors, equating outworn devices, behaviors, and lifestyles with stodginess.

Often, just looking older translates to "need not apply." Unfortunately, violation of the Age Discrimination Act is hard to prove, and those who feel the discrimination rarely have the wherewithal to fight, feeling that even if they win, their victory will be hollow and they will not be welcome in the place they had to sue. If you are just entering your sixties, you may already have been made aware, painfully, that, along with racism, sexism, and other flaws in the fabric of our society, ageism ranks right up there with obstacles you may be facing. A lot depends, of course, on the kind of work you've been doing—even sometimes on where you live and work and how you have upgraded your own skills. A lot also depends on the stereotypes you have probably absorbed about older people and that you may even be applying, unconsciously, to yourself.

A man is sitting on the side of the bed in his pajamas, staring. His wife says, "What are you doing?" He says, "Trying to remember whether I was getting up or going to bed."

Funny? We've got dozens more. You probably know lots of jokes about aging, sometimes referred to as "gallows humor" or "whistling past the graveyard." Fear is often most potently handled, and masked, by humor. No one we met would give up the ability to laugh about aging. Nor would we. At least, not about ourselves. It's certainly better, for both mental and physical health, to laugh than to cry. There is plenty of scientific research that tells us that the same endorphins that result in response to exercise, excitement, love, and orgasm seem to be triggered by laughter. It's even been demonstrated in research that the ability to withstand physical pain is greater following laughter (watching fifteen minutes of comedy in a group) than following something that doesn't make you laugh. Maybe because those abdominal muscles relax when we laugh.

Okay! A few more:

Three old guys are out walking. First one says, "Windy, isn't it?" Second one says, "No, it's Thursday!" Third one says, "So am I. Let's go get a beer."

"I just got a state-of-the-art hearing aid. It cost $3,000, but it's great!" "What kind is it?" "Twelve-thirty."

This old gentleman was out driving, both hands grasping the wheel in
a vise-like grip, his eyes peering over the dashboard, when his grand-
daughter called on the cell phone.

"Grandpop! I saw on TV that some lunatic is driving the wrong way
on the freeway, so I wanted to warn you to watch out!"

Grandpop's eyes quickly darted out of the left side window and then
out of the right as he shouts back into the phone, "One lunatic? There
are hundreds of them."

Ouch! All funny, but the first noticeable signs that you're no longer
the invincible Man of Steel you used to be can be alarming. Was forgetting where you put the keys a sign of Alzheimer's? Fears about becoming
doddering and losing one's senses are the most common sources of jokes,
not to mention the growing realization that it may no longer be safe to
drive. This one strikes at the heart of the boy inside who prized learning
to drive right up there with every other meaningful rite of passage. More
than any other mark of manhood, driving meant independence and freedom. You probably gave your first car a name. Give that up?? Oh, the
trauma! Actually, it turns out that we're on the cusp of an era when
driving one's own car shows signs of losing its iconic status in the lives of
many, especially city dwellers who are finding Uber the lower-cost alter-
native to maintaining a car in the city, and self-driving automobiles are
not far off.

Then again, when we stop giggling at ourselves and get serious, we do
need to notice that there are glaring exceptions and alarming downsides
to the chuckles about aging.

Stop here for a moment and think:

- Have you been hearing those jokes since you were a child?
- Have you been absorbing those stereotypes since you were a child?
- Did you assume that all "elders" shared the same infirmities, loss of
  memory, hearing loss, and judgment about their own lives as someone in your family?
- Are you still focused on the negative possibilities of aging and
  unaware of the opportunities for growth and change?

These were powerful images and attitudes to absorb when you had no
need to find them frightening, or to defend against or question them. Well

absorbed over a lifetime, these negative beliefs have been found to persist and influence our self-perceptions as we ourselves age. In fact, they may have planted seeds of condescension and arrogance in knowing they didn't in any way apply to you, the young and strong person. The expectation of all kinds of diminishment has even been shown to weaken the will to live and take years off of life. Dr. Becca Levy's ongoing research on stereotypes is groundbreaking.[1] She is credited with creating a field of study that focuses on how positive and negative age stereotypes, which are assimilated from the culture, can have beneficial and adverse effects, respectively, on the health of older individuals. Her studies have been conducted by longitudinal, experimental, and cross-cultural methods. The stereotypes are reinforced daily in the media and in real life situations.

Author's Note: I remember vividly when my mother was in her early nineties, living independently in an apartment house for seniors, and how delighted she was when a large contingent of new renters moved in. Mother told me she was so happy because they were Chinese and she knew they would appreciate her for her age. She was reluctant to share her age with most contemporaries who had their own discriminatory hierarchy within the building, based on age. However, she loved telling young people who asked because she felt it was "good for them to know you could be old and still have a good conversation."

Herbert G., whom you will meet soon again in chapter 2, is at ninety-five a man of experience, wisdom, and excellent judgment. He has a very good mutually respectful relationship with his internist. When he was referred for further examination to a cardiologist, one of his daughters asked to go with him. Although he felt it wasn't necessary, Herbert knew that going with him would make her feel better; he even admitted that another pair of caring, alert eyes and ears are a really good thing at important doctor visits. Both Herbert and his daughter were offended when the doctor addressed almost all of his comments and even his questions to the daughter, rather than to the patient. The assumption prompted Herbert's admonishment to the doctor.

> *I suggested, in a kindly way, that he not assume dementia because of my age and that he understand that my hearing aids make me perfectly capable of hearing speech at a moderate level. And that I was the patient and my daughter was the observer.*

We've all heard of the overzealous Boy Scout who kept helping older people cross the street, whether they wanted to go there or not. Funny image, right? With the best of intentions, that is exactly what many people do. To someone already grappling with the realization that they are suddenly being treated with condescension by many people they encounter, even by family members, the offer of help crossing the street may elicit a cranky response, like hitting the Boy Scout over the head with one's cane. That would be fighting back against the stereotype in the extreme, of course, and would surely hurt the boy's feelings. But you understand the point: evidence of a physical disability or of aging is no reason to assume loss of judgment, loss of intelligence, or loss of decision-making authority.

With the exception of a few professional fields—notably, academia, science, the arts, and government—ageism remains prevalent in the workplace. It becomes more evident in retirement, however, in social situations, including family events for many, even for those who continue to flourish professionally well into older age. Being seen as irrelevant, ignored in conversations, or otherwise treated with condescension comes as a shock, more likely to be administered by the next generation down than by their children. Just watch; it will happen! Staying informed, keeping relevant, and being an interested, respectful listener is up to the retiree. License to lecture is not granted with advancing age. (You will meet **Govind T.**, known as **Dada**, in chapter 2, who teaches not by speech but by example.)

AGING VERSUS AGEISM

Dealing with the physical side of aging actually requires the kind of intelligence and wisdom that only growing up as well as growing older can bring (see chapter 7). There have always been, however, those who are determined to put off the inevitable rather than face and make the most of it. In *The Human Values in Aging Newsletter*, editor Harry R. Moody asked and answered the following question: *Why don't we get rid of aging?*[2]

> *When I taught gerontology, I used to tell my students that no one had ever found any intervention to delay the biological process of aging or*

extend maximum human life span. Mme. Jeanne Calment lived to 122 years, but no one has been able to surpass that. I also told them that calorie restriction did extend the healthy life span of almost all animals on which it was used: trials with primates were still underway. Alas, since then, it has not been found to work with primates (that's us, folks). It gives new meaning to the old joke, "Doctor, if I follow your low-calorie diet, will I live longer, or will it just seem longer?"

Yet hope springs eternal for the fountain of youth. Now no less than Google (rebranded Alphabet Inc.) is investing serious money in a "moon-shot" approach to finding a cause, and cure, for aging. The company plans to invest up to $750 million in this effort through its venture company Calico. Google is not the only company in the game. Craig Venter, the man who cracked the code of the human genome, has his own enterprise, Human Longevity, Inc., aiming to unlock the genetic code and enable people to live longer. Americans are not alone in the quest. British Aubrey de Grey aims to "end aging as we have known it," enabling us to live a thousand years or more. His SENS Research Foundation promotes rejuvenation research of all kinds.

Is any of this possible? No one really knows. Human beings had longed for heavier-than-air flight for centuries. By the early twentieth century many scientists claimed it was impossible—until two bicycle makers (the Wright brothers) flew into the air at Kitty Hawk and proved them wrong. On the other hand, it has also been said that "controlled hydrogen fusion power is twenty years in the future and always has been."

I conclude by noting that I have three personal friends who are now dead after taking (against my advice) human growth hormone and later dying of cancer. Antiaging products on the market today are a snare and a delusion. Yet more MDs are now members of the American Academy of Anti-Aging Medicine than there are board-certified geriatricians in this country. Someone needs to ask, "What's wrong with this picture?"

Embracing or, at the very least, accepting *aging* means rejecting age*ism*. It means that you understand that you have earned every emerging line in your face, every lost or graying hair, and every nascent ache in your limbs. It means that you, unlike others who haven't made it this far in life, are still acquiring experience and the opportunity for wisdom and new adventures that go with it. It means that, rather than focusing on what others may think they are losing, you focus on what is opening up for you. *It means not buying into an emerging stereotype that new, exciting ideas come only from the young.* It takes the ultimate "manning up" and earns the biggest payoff: this is the time of your ultimate growth and opportunity as a human being—that is, a Man.

IS IT POSSIBLE TO KEEP UP WITH
THE CHANGES IN MY WORLD? IN MYSELF?

In conversations with men from all walks of life, from retired police and firefighters, to college professors and businesspeople, from artists and doctors to spiritual seekers, and so many in between, we learned that men are doing more than facing the challenges that accompany aging; they are living in newly fulfilling ways every day. They're finding that their goals change as they grow older and that there is opportunity to really grow up, not merely grow old. They let us know their specific concerns: identity, relationship adjustments with partners that come with changes in working (or nonworking) schedules, finding new interests and reviving old passions, discovering and resolving sex and intimacy issues, recognizing depression and dealing with it if it occurs, living through separation and loss, navigating the health industry, recognizing who they are and can be, maintaining their place in the family, living in a digital world, and isolation. Their stories, in their own words, are here. They come from the Greatest Generation and the boomers. And, oh, yes, you will even find the perspective of one Millennial who's looking ahead. You have your own story. If the way forward looks bumpy, they're here to help and inspire.

BUT MEN DON'T TALK . . . OR DO THEY?

We were surprised to find openness and even eagerness to share experiences and observations that we had been warned would be unlikely. Men, we were told, don't like to talk about feelings. Many, we found, were like **Bob R.** in Mill Valley, California, who first retired at fifty-five, twenty-five years ago. Bob described several close male friends with whom he plays golf and works on various projects.

If you have a problem, or are worried about something, would you talk it over with one of them? What do you talk about with your close male friends?

> *Oh, no—I wouldn't talk my problems over with them. I'd talk to Wanda, not one of the guys. When I talk to the guys we talk about sports, news, things we're working on. I can relax, play golf, have a few beers with them sometimes.*

Wanda is Bob's ex-wife and still his friend.

Talking about personal matters and feelings was often, we learned, easier for men with a woman than with male friends. Those who were married usually regarded their wives as their only real confidants rather than their male friends. Men who lose or have no partner often become isolated, we found.

Several years back, staff at the Riverdale Senior Center in New York noticed that women who came to their center for meals and activities seemed naturally to gather in impromptu discussions while men either clung to their wives or sat by themselves (if they had come alone). A retired doctor, who became part of a men's group (sixty and up) that was soon established, noted that "the average woman has several friends, while the average man has one—a wife or girlfriend—and if he loses her, he's up a creek." Having a male facilitator, they found, made all the difference when the group was formed, and men gathered to speak freely about their concerns, which generally centered on "relationships, sex, and money." The opportunity to open up in unfamiliar ways has kept the group viable and important to its members to this day. When we met with nineteen of the Riverdale Senior Center men in the Bronx, we found them eager to let us know how important being in the group is to them, how much they value the time they spend together, and what an anchor it has become in their lives.

It took a long time for the group at Riverdale to come together. It took a long time to realize that sharing experiences and ideas about life with other men is more than okay. It's a good thing, even if it is new and unfamiliar to so many men used to "manning up" to life's challenges. A changing trend, however, can be seen among younger men. (More about that later.)

ROLLING (OR NOT) WITH CULTURAL CHANGE

Having lived through rapid changes in the world they inhabit, men who reach what used to be traditional retirement age are seeing their children expect to change occupations to a degree previously unimagined. They are seeing examples of adaptability to change among younger men in the marketplace and in society. These examples present opportunities for open-minded fathers and grandfathers as well. Rolling with the changes, the older generation realize, isn't exemplified by always displaying an apparent three-day growth of facial hair but by having an open mind to what the younger men may have to teach them about resilience.

One of the most dramatic changes, in terms of time and institutions, has been in attitudes and laws regarding homosexuality. The men you will meet in these pages made it clear, for the most part, that their attitudes toward homosexuality reflect the sea change in modern society, ranging from (rarely stated) indifference to clear approval of same-sex marriage. Both straight and gay men offered unsolicited opinions in our conversations, usually based on personal experience within their families as they realized that the children they raised and love were gay. *Transgender* was a word they mostly never heard or seldom read when they were growing up. Some revealed that they had surprised themselves by their acceptance of a new norm.

Most of us take the use of our computers and the incorporation of the Internet and social media into our lives for granted at this point. But, with the exception of the youngest person in this book (and Joe V., below), these were new concepts at one point to everyone else we encountered. Having lived through this monumental change, take a moment to contemplate how communication and accessing information has changed since you were in school. Take another moment to reflect on how you have learned skills that seemed daunting to many of us at first and how this technology affects your life and opportunities today.

Not all the men we interviewed have embraced the Internet, however, which was unexpected. **Joe V.**, a retired policeman, sees no need for it in his life, which centers now on caregiving for a developmentally disabled brother-in-law, being the mainstay for his diabetic six-year-old grand-daughter, and assisting his still-employed policewoman wife and "true partner in life." He reckons he may have to tune in, however, as his granddaughter moves into elementary school.

NO TEXTBOOK HERE

Academic, scientific study is not what this book is about. Instead, we found men who ranged in age from sixty-one to one hundred who share their stories in their own words. Our antennae were alert. These men were recommended by people we knew or came from chance encounters. From eighth-grade dropouts to doctors of medicine, dentistry, and philosophy, they appreciated the opportunity to share not only what they've experienced and learned but also what they are still learning. Part of growing up along with growing older appears to be awareness that there is value in sharing hard-earned wisdom and remaining or becoming part of a larger community.

In every case, our "interviews" were less structured interviews than they were lengthy conversations, which often took us in unexpected places. It was surprising to us, for example, to have several of the men remark, unasked, and almost verbatim, "I know that I'm not as attractive to women as I once was." (They were all still handsome, by the way.)

Sometimes it's serendipity at work, like the day **Curry G.**, a 6'5" gentle giant in his mid-thirties, came to install a phone in my office and he and I got to talking. He noticed a copy of *The New Senior Woman* on my desk and asked, "Is that yours? Are you a writer?" When I told him that we were working on the book about *The New Senior Man*, Curry urged me to talk to his pastor. He went on to tell me that he, himself, was having a difficult time going through a divorce and custody problems. He was missing his children a lot, he said, and was finding help and support through a men's group at his church. Curry said he was surprised to find how much the group was helping him cope with a difficult time. Being in a group that talks about feelings is old hat for most women; they can create a support network in a heartbeat and form deep and lasting emotional bonds over lunch with a new friend. But men? This is a rather new and growing phenomenon, especially for older men, even those with close pals linked through a shared history, sports, politics, or other interests. And that was our link to **Keith Walker**, a pastor and director of men's, women's and singles' ministries at the LCBC megachurch in Manheim, Pennsylvania, and several other sites around Lancaster County.

What have you found, Keith?

At sixty-two, ordained in 1976 and married for several decades, Keith has had years of experience with boys and men, including his own four sons and now three grandsons. Keith has spoken and worked with groups of mixed ages and of young men all around the world. He had a lot to tell us on the subject of manhood from his vantage point:

> *Men for generations now have not been taught how to be men. A man is someone protecting the hearts of those around him. A room will always be better when a man walks in than when he doesn't. That's true of our culture.*
>
> *For years I spoke to high school– and college-age students all around the world. That was always my passion. About fifteen years ago I realized that, if I'm really going to change these amazing students that I get a chance to talk to, I really need to impact their fathers, who have been absent for a pretty long time period and in many ways. We've gone through an interesting history where 120 years ago every young man worked with his dad. They either worked on a farm or in a trade together, for the most part. When the Industrial Revolution hit, our fathers went off to work before the sun came up until the sun went down, giving the best part of their lives to someone other than their families. Boys became disconnected with their dads.*
>
> *At the end of the Second World War, the fathers Tom Brokaw called "the greatest generation" had emotionally shut down. They stopped sharing their emotions. All of a sudden, the three things a man needs to hear from his dad—"I love you," "I'm proud of you," "this is what you're good at"—were missing. There was no verbalization of love, of real support. Not because these guys were jerks. They had just seen things. Emotionally they felt that the best way to deal with what they were feeling was to just go quiet.*
>
> *And then the women's movement hit in the seventies. It was critical that this should happen in response to incredible inequality, but our culture interpreted that as men and women being the same.*

Are they not?

It's a misunderstanding to think that being equal means being the same. We're not. We're wired differently. All of a sudden guys became very confused. They're not hearing from their dads how to connect physically or emotionally, and they don't even know how to respond to the opposite sex. Everything became very confused, and we had a very self-absorbed generation of men. [The influence of] pornography exemplifies the kind of twisted thought process some men go through—where instead of having relationships, we have something we use; we have objects. I do see evidence of positive change, however. For example, when my oldest son had a great opportunity offered him by his employer, we talked it over. It involved moving, and his primary concern was how that would affect his family—his wife and children. I think that represents a difference between today and earlier days, when men mainly or completely considered their own career development.

When Keith describes the program Curry first told me about, it becomes clear that in the twenty-four weeks a successful participant will have developed something that is so often lacking in men's lives. This is how Keith describes it:

We meet with our guys once a week for twenty-four weeks. We always say the first six weeks are deciding if they want to leave. This year my group ranges from a young teenager to eighty-seven. As the course progresses by design, a member becomes part of a cohort of eight to ten guys in his same life stage. Over the twenty-four weeks, they develop trust, first by telling something to someone they thought they trusted and eventually telling something they thought they'd never tell anyone. When that happens, they've bonded for life. It takes guys that long to develop that trust.

We tend to put guys together so they can walk through the experiences together, not feeling they have to mentor each other so much as "Let's talk this through together." We teach them concepts, and they break into groups to immediately talk about them. At our church in the last eleven years since we started this I've taught about ten thousand guys.

What do you hope they learn?

> *There's a certain phase in a man's life we call the "sage phase." It's after cowboy; it's after warrior, lover, king. It's after all the phases, and "sage" is where you really begin to get it, what is important. We always tell our guys, "I've never been with a guy at his deathbed where he talks about his toys." That's not what does it for us. He talks about his relationships, how he wishes he had spent more time with certain people or certain experiences. I tell our guys, "Find your pallbearers now. Find the guys to carry your casket now, and do life with them. They're the guys who are the most important in your world."*

DOES "MANNING UP" HAVE A NEW MEANING?

The old connotation of manning up strongly implied that facing whatever you had to man up to was best done alone—and definitely best left unsaid. After all, wasn't the iconic image of the hero, imprinted thousands of times on our subconscious, someone riding off into the sunset alone? The New Senior Man sometimes knows better. He may even have a friend to confide in—not just to tell whom he voted for or which team he follows. He may even be part of a group that finds support and inspiration in digging into feelings and experiences previously kept inside, when another man's view might be worth hearing and might awaken him to possibilities he hadn't thought of. The concept of manhood itself has been through definitions and redefinitions before, notably after the Civil War and after the turn of the twentieth century, between and following the world wars.[3] You, the New Senior Man, are living through a period of redefinition at what seems like lightning speed with the advantages of time and possibilities of how to make the most of it your forefathers never knew. Lucky you! That's why you're the *New* Senior Man.

EVIDENCE OF AGING WELL EXISTS

A well-known study of how people age well does exist. We are fortunate to have ongoing results of the longest such research project in the world: The Study of Adult Development is now in its eighth decade and is known also as the Grant Study for its original funding by the William T. Grant Foundation. Directed by Dr. George E. Vaillant at Harvard Medical School, the study has followed a group of Harvard men who were sophomores from the classes of 1939 through 1944, along with the Glueck Study, supervised by Dr. Vaillant, which included disadvantaged inner-city youths who grew up in Boston between 1940 and 1945. In his book *Aging Well*, as well as in subsequent published articles and observations, Dr. Vaillant has helped us realize that the old notion of peaking in middle age and then declining doesn't hold up.[4]

Most encouraging, perhaps, is the amount of evidence needed to confirm that healthy, positive aspects of aging are attained even when people have survived what appear to be insurmountable difficulties. One of the poor inner-city boys in Dr. Vaillant's study who had such difficulties but achieved a very successful and fulfilling older age is presented as an example of someone who "was not a prisoner of his childhood; he gave to his children what he could not have himself; he loved his wife for fifty years; and he never felt sick, even when he was ill." "Not a prisoner of his childhood" is worthy of repetition and contemplation. Recognizing and accepting what is past appears to be part of moving on with the spirit needed in order to continue to grow, to thrive, and discover new strengths. Child development is over; senior development is evident in each of the men whose stories you will find here. From the man whose first opera was written and produced in his eighth decade to the early-retired teacher who follows his dream as a voice-over artist to the electronics technician who surprises himself as he finds fellowship and a sense of peace in being part of a group, each is an original, yet an example of reinvention and renewal.

The importance of role models is underscored in Dr. Vaillant's advice. "Old age," he says, "is like a minefield: if you see footprints leading to the other side, step in them."

Later adult development, according to Dr. Vaillant and the several noted researchers he references, can no longer be thought of as a time of loss of physical strength and agility or beauty or a loss of productiveness or energy or mental acuity. Rather, it is now seen for what it can be and for most of us is: a continuing stage in human development. In the last two decades of life, he sees the critical components as, "first, being ill without feeling sick; second, regaining a capacity for creativity and play in retirement; third, the acquisition of wisdom; and, fourth, the cultivation of spirituality."

LEGACY

We asked the men we interviewed what place legacy has in their thinking. Many quickly, and surprisingly, said, "None." We soon realized how misleading that first negative response was. Almost everyone dismissed any (expressed) concern about legacy in material terms, but further discussion usually revealed conscious wishes to be remembered well, to be seen as having done one's best for the people he cares about most or for the larger society. They may not regard it as legacy, but how men live, how they rise to challenges, how they develop their own best ideas, how they relate to their families, how they never stop learning and growing not only fulfills their own lives but also makes them role models for each other and those who will follow. *Thinking about legacy focuses the mind on the why of your life.*

HALF FULL OR HALF EMPTY?

If you were smart enough to buy this book, congratulations! If someone loves you enough to have bought it for you, lucky you! You're reading it now, so you're already on your way to creating your own successful, fulfilling "retirement" years. "Retirement" is in quotation marks because the overwhelming answer given by the many men we interviewed in writing this book when we asked "What advice would you give to someone contemplating retirement?" was *"Don't do it!"* Their fuller responses, as you will learn as you meet these men in coming chapters, varied widely. All acknowledged that, in a world so different from the one their fathers and grandfathers inhabited, the concept of retirement is definitely not what it used to be. Instead, it is becoming a stage of life rather than a condition defined by the limitations of formal employment: a stage of life with more options and more opportunities than men in earlier generations imagined. The challenges and limitations aging can bring still require courage and adjustments that echo their fathers'. Whether you regard this stage as one that is half full or half empty can make all the difference in the world. Attitude change is possible, if you need it!

You will learn much about some and something about all of the men we talked with as they share their experiences and observations throughout the book. After you've met Bob or Theo or Tom in more than one or two places, you'll begin to feel you know them. They were all eager to communicate with you through us.

Meeting people who are living the half-full version of retirement is inspiring—not because they can or should be imitated but because they can spark your own ideas. Role models provide evidence that growth need not stop, or even slow down, when everything else seems to. Instead, these men show us that countless different paths are possible and that new directions lead us to even greater places than we might have thought we were heading. They make us grateful for this gift of time and knowledge that eluded previous generations. Recognizing that time is a gift is half the battle. Game on! You're already winning just by being here.

2

WHO AM I NOW THAT I'M RETIRED?

Be sure that whatever you are is you.

—Theodore Roethke

Remember you? Stop here for a minute. Go take a look in the mirror. You really still are the same guy underneath that graying (or not), receding (or not) head of hair, that clean shave (or the whatever-is-fashionable facial-hair growth). The brain is still ticking along, actually filled with more than you may appreciate at the moment. If your vision is a little less clear, or your hearing not quite as sharp, take heart! You're living in a time when most oncoming signs of frailty are easily remedied and compensated for. (Hearing aids are state-of-the-art and virtually invisible.) You have all the best attributes of the old you (count 'em), and if you're one of those men who experiences what feels like an identity crisis, you will not only find yourself again but also discover that the self you find will be even better than you ever expected.

I'VE HAD MY COFFEE AND READ THE NEWSPAPER. NOW WHAT?

This was precisely the question asked by **Arthur S.** of Baltimore, Maryland, while we were chatting over coffee in a diner. We both had attended a library lecture, where we happened to be sitting next to each other, and struck up a conversation. Arthur told me he liked to read and had decided to attend the library lecture that morning. But this was really just a time killer, he told me, and not too satisfying intellectually. He confessed to being a recent retiree and spending most of his time incredibly bored. I invited him to tell me more.

Well, I still awake to my alarm clock every morning. It's one habit I can't seem to break. I still put my watch on the counter in the bathroom, shower, shave, and dress. Only now I no longer wear a suit and tie. I go down to breakfast, read the paper, and at 11 a.m. plan the rest of my day. But that's where the emptiness begins to loom large. I'm forced to confront the fact that there are many hours left in the day and every day the hours seem longer. Sometimes I have a project around the house to complete. Sometimes I have a doctor's or a lawyer's appointment. But on most days, I don't have a plan. And, believe it or not, I almost panic. I read and I play golf, but that's not enough. Golf twice a week is enough. More than that is boring, not to mention very expensive!

But here's what's eating me. I have three grown children. My eldest son is quite successful, has a working wife, and I can't believe what he's done. He has quit his perfectly good job to stay at home and raise his daughter! He says he's not worried that it will ruin his career. He's not embarrassed to go shopping or pick her up at day care with the other parents [women] or hang out at the playground with my granddaughter. I'm embarrassed for him when I have to tell people that he's a househusband. I wonder if he's a real guy! Here I am, struggling with retirement after a long working life in a successful business, and he's decided to "retire" in his forties. But he says it's only for about ten years. I just don't get it.

We'll hear more from Arthur later. But first let's dissect his quandary. Arthur's situation is not unique. He has two problems: First, Arthur doesn't seem to have the resources to make his retirement years as rewarding as his life had been up to this point. Second, he hasn't come to terms with the fact that his son's perspective on life may be—in fact, *is*—different from his. Not of less value, just different.

MAYBE I SHOULD HAVE SEEN THIS COMING!

Arthur started to prepare for his adult life when he was a small child. People asked him what he wanted to be when he grew up, and he knew he'd better have an answer. As he grew up, he knew that he was headed for college, probably marriage, a home of his own, and a job in which he would succeed, making a living so that he could take care of his family. Arthur did it all—and did it well. Arthur's is a success story. But while he was making all that happen, did he plan for his retirement? Probably not.

Arthur's parents and the generation that preceded his didn't expect long years of retirement, perhaps another third of their lifetime, many years of good health, vitality, and the means—perhaps small, but fixed and reliable—and the ability (at the very least through the Internet) to remain involved in the world. In a way, Arthur and the rest of his generation born during the 1930s and 1940s were blindsided by this bonanza of good fortune. Arthur was, and maybe still is, always worried that tomorrow may bring stormy weather and he must be prepared with a raincoat and galoshes. So maybe he wasn't prepared for the fact that when he retired in his early sixties he would enter a whole new stage of life, that he might have thirty years of vigorous living ahead of him.

Preparation for retirement usually focuses on financial planning and security. And with good reason. A financially secure life is a lot happier than an insecure one. There's money to be made here by advisors in the financial industry, and, of course, they've risen to the challenge. However, emotional security in this stage of life is of equal importance; sadly, this issue is not so energetically addressed. Often, men who have been happiest and most successful in their work lives have conflated their commitment to their work, even their titles or job descriptions, with their very identity, and society conspires by invariably asking "What do you do?" when a man is introduced. "Who am I?" is a serious question when the work identity is no more.

What does it take to make the most of these retirement years when real change is needed? To make them meaningful, rewarding, stimulating, exciting? To also meet the challenges that will inevitably be experienced? There will be losses and diminishing health, energy, and reserves, even as longevity and medical miracles increase. Arthur has perhaps not contemplated the complexities, the opportunities, the trials that are ahead of him. There is work to be done!

DIFFERENT STROKES FOR DIFFERENT FOLKS

Arthur's son Jeffrey's is a different narrative. Jeffrey, born in the 1950s or 1960s, was raised to expect that all good things in life are his right. He was neither scarred nor scared by the Great Depression, World War II, or even the war in Vietnam. His were parents who lavished praise and made sure that he would build up great self-esteem. And so he grew up with a sense of entitlement. He feels entitled to happiness, a safe place in the middle class, and the freedom to shape his life as he wishes. Jeffrey expects that his wife will work and that he won't have sole responsibility for earning the family's living. Jeffrey may not even know what galoshes are! Blessed with a sunny disposition and a lack of arrogance, despite what some might consider an overindulged upbringing, Jeffrey is an easy-going, pleasant guy.

However, Jeffrey has not done anything to prepare for retirement. Are his expectations different from his father's? Yes, in some respects. Both he and his wife were happy for him to take on the household and child-rearing chores for a time with no loss of self-respect to either one. Their views about male and female roles are much more flexible than Arthur's and allow them more latitude in how they manage their lives. These liberal attitudes toward their roles represent a generational change that we've noticed in men of different age groups whom we've interviewed. The one thing that crosses generations is the uncertainty of what life will be like when the workday is no longer the structure that holds the week together.

How Jeffrey will view his decision to be a househusband can only be known a few years from now. But we were able talk to **Bruce G.** of Petaluma, California, who chose a path similar to Jeffrey's. Bruce was a firefighter and retired at age fifty-four. The family had a dilemma:

> *I was very fortunate in that Edie, my wife, and I both worked for CAL FIRE. Summertime, just like this summer in California, is crazy because of the intensity and longevity of the wildfire, and we happen to be wildland firefighters. It's not uncommon for firefighters to leave home and not come back for weeks—almost like military service. You go out on an assignment and come back when the assignment is done, and some of these fires can go on for two to three weeks at a time.*

> *We had a son, and we may have had more children but life was difficult in the summer. It was a strain to have childcare. I probably*

would have worked a couple of more years, but Edie was still working. Our son was in eighth grade, and you know how teenagers are. We worried about him constantly. I had the opportunity to retire with good benefits, and the childcare situation was getting even more difficult because of the prolonged wildfires that summer. So I think it was a blessing to be able to retire at that time.

But when I took parental leave—it was available in California—my colleagues at work were aghast! Firefighting is such a male-dominated field, and a male being a nanny is just not right.

So I never got any pressure from my parents, but I did from my colleagues. My supervisor said I ruined any chances for promotions because of this. I was upset by this because I knew I was doing the right thing, and I said some things I shouldn't have said, but the bottom line was it was the best decision of my life.

Pressure from his colleagues! Complicating this issue of retirement are social pressures. In Jeffrey's case, parental pressures. In other cases, we've seen pressures from a wife whose ideas about her husband's role differed from his (see chapter 6). Bruce is a fortunate guy. He is his own man and manned up to retirement as he saw it and so withstood the pressures—in this case, the contempt of his colleagues. When his son no longer needed him at home, Bruce went into "real" retirement.

It was like a long vacation. I was euphoric with all that free time. No worries about work. Life was a "beach." But after a month, I realized nobody cares about me. I went into a mini-depression. It was like nobody cares that I'm not coming into work! They're doing it all without me. So what is my purpose in life? And I had a purpose the first few years of retirement. But now . . .

Bruce, however, is on his way to solving the issues that he now realizes he is facing in retirement. He is being proactive about, first, recognizing that there's work to be done on the transitional issues in his life and, second, the admission that he's not the same guy he was before he stopped working.

Dealing with adjustments in one's identity can be one of life's greatest emotional challenges. A major dilemma becomes, at this stage of life, "Who am I"—not *what* but *who*. Most people spend the first part of their lives, from the time they are children through adolescence and young adulthood, planning for adulthood, planning for the "what." And then they spend the bulk of their lives *being* adults. But how much thought do people give to planning for retirement? Life past midlife can encompass as much as a third of one's life; yet preparation for this stage is the exception rather than the norm.

A sample of the research seems to indicate that when people *do* think about retirement they tend to focus on financial planning rather than on emotional issues. Retirement dreams are vague. According to the Transamerica Center for Retirement Studies, most people include traveling, spending more time with the family, and pursuing hobbies as plans for retirement.[1] The reality, though, is that families are frequently spread out and less frequently visited, many working men have no hobbies, and the time at home is often spent wondering what to do with all this time. The most frequently cited retirement fear, the center reports, among workers of all ages is "outliving my savings and investments."

But there are many unspoken fears. Men often don't want to share their feelings or may have limited vocabularies to express them. Many men have spent most of their lives competing with others in the workplace and on athletic fields, starting at preschool playgrounds, where little boys' groups are (self-)hierarchically organized and power relationships are recognized, while girls' groups are more based on personal friendships or relationships—that is, affiliative.[2] Men seem to have difficulty acknowledging vulnerability and weakness, often viewing this as a flaw in their masculinity and something that needs to be kept secret. Many men come to retirement without a network of friends outside the workplace.

AM I THE SAME GUY?

Well, actually, you're not. Your life has changed. When you walk into a room full of new people, they don't know how important you were, how in control you were of your life, or what a great guy you are. It was the same when you were a boy, especially a teenager who went to a new school. The other kids regarded you with suspicion, wanted to know who you really were before they let you in to the group. Here is **Alfred Stillman** of Philadelphia, Pennsylvania, from whom you will hear again later. But here is what he found when he offered his very valuable medical services to a few community-volunteer organizations:

> *Now that I no longer work full time I'm very interested in volunteering my extra time. I want to work, and I don't care if I don't get paid. I have had a rewarding medical career, a life of service, and I want to continue that. I phoned more than one community-volunteer organization and left messages. I was never called back. Finally I just gave up. If they aren't interested enough to phone me back, I'm not interested in them. I think that's an indication of their lack of commitment and inefficiency, and I don't want to work for them.*

Well, hold on, there, Alfred. Let's think about those volunteer agencies you called. Their phones are probably manned by volunteers, perhaps a different one each day. They may never have been professional receptionists in their former lives nor had jobs where those skills were required. Perhaps the message never got to the right person to process your request. Perhaps that person, also a volunteer, lost the message. Yes, many volunteer agencies may be inefficient, so it can be a hard climb to get to where you can make the difference we know you will make once you get there. You really are the same guy. The context has been changing.

TRANSITION

Once you retire, are you the same guy? You may be the same guy in your own eyes, but your life is changing you into a new person in some ways. Your network of friends was probably all the people you dealt with daily at work: your colleagues, your employees, your employers, your clients, your tennis buddies, depending on your situation. Except for your golf or tennis partner, you probably will not see much of your old network and will have to form a new one. You probably don't have a whole lot of experience at that. In most households, the social events are managed by the wife or partner. How often did you make the arrangements and mark them on the calendar? That may still work for you for activities that you do together, but what about the many hours you will be spending apart? You will probably have to find your own *new* network of friends.

This is not easy to do. You won't like everyone who may at first seem like someone you want to connect with. What seems like a fit when you're desperate to make one may not be a fit after all. It takes time to get to know each other. And it doesn't help to tell how important you were in your former life. You're in a new life now, and you have to prove yourself all over again. You have to come off to people as a nice guy to be with.

Sadly, some men cannot make the transition comfortably from working stiff to retired senior. They become unhappy and bored. Unhappiness breeds anger and bitterness, and then these men look for external reasons for their unhappiness. That's when the complaints gush forth. Everything, petty and big, becomes the object of their ire. "Is everything all right?" asked by the people who serve their needs becomes "Is anything all right?" There is a cohort of retirees whose main interaction is with other bored and unhappy retirees. Their fun comes from complaining. However, this is not the usual story. More often, they sit at home, watch television or read until their eyes glaze over, and get depressed. Many men don't like to admit to such an unmacho response to their situations, so they don't do anything about it. We'll deal with that in a later chapter.

The trick here is to avoid these pitfalls. We've met many men who have!

Meet **Govind T.**, known affectionately to all at Peace Village in New York as **Dada**. He was born on March 31,1926, in Chidambaram, Tamil Nadu, in the south of India.

I came to the United States from India in 1987 and went back and forth until 1999 when my wife became ill. We went back to Mumbai, where I took complete care of her until she died. I came back to the US to stay with my daughter. I also have one son and two grandsons, eleven and thirteen. I have a PhD in chemistry and worked in a factory doing research and development. I retired in 1987. For a few months I was out of sorts because I didn't know what to do, but I took up some voluntary work for a year or two. We had a house in India, so I stayed here for six months and there for six months. A few years before I retired, we got into the spiritual life. I became interested in Brahma Kumaris. I've been doing yoga for forty years. Towards the end of my service, I got into yoga asanas for my exercise, which are different postures from yoga—less vigorous.

Tell me about your day, Dada.

I get up every morning at 3 a.m.. At 3:20 or 3:25 I come to Baba's room, for five minutes to one hour for meditation. [Baba's room is a sanctuary devoted to Dada Lekhraj Kripalani, an ordinary human being who achieved greatness by rising to the challenge of the deeper truths of life. He is revered by Brahma Kumaris.] We call that Amrit Velā. I go back to my room and do my morning rituals—shower, et cetera—then I start yoga asanas for forty-five minutes to an hour. Then I go for a half hour to forty-five-minute walk. I need a walker for that now, but I accommodate to my diminishing strength without giving up what is important to me. Before 6 a.m. I do these things. At 6 all the people who live here at Peace Village come together to class where we meditate and then have spiritual discourse. At 7:45, we have breakfast. At 8 or 8:30 a.m. I am free. Since I came here, I have not missed a day. Before that, I was sick often. Now, no more.

In the afternoon I take a nap. When I wake up I write letters and have frequent phone conversations connecting to my family in India; I read about the world. This is how I keep in touch. We have no television here. But I have many contacts—the Internet, people, books, newspapers, magazines—to keep me informed. My big interest is classical music, and I pursue that. I also paint. I feel as though I couldn't pack more into twenty-four hours.

You have not been sick since you've been following this ritual?

No, I've had lots of physical problems—I had a heart bypass five years ago—and I take a fistful of pills. There is a big difference between pain and suffering. Because I follow this discipline, my mind is off the pain. This discipline has kept me going. The only way to fight the pain is to keep the routine. When I'm in pain I go into Baba's room and meditate. Thinking about my soul keeps my mind off my body. God is always ready to give you strength. It is up to you to take it.

As the elder statesman in this community, what advice do you give to the younger men? So many younger people fear becoming older.

I set an example not by speech or talking. Many people have come in contact with me and stayed in my home. They tell me they are learning a lot of things from me. They see what I do morning and night. By my example I inculcate my teaching. They see that I am strong, I am

*happy. By being active at my age they tell me that I set an example. All
my life I have led by example. In raising my children and now here at
Peace Village. People thought when I came here at eighty that I was
finished. I showed them that I am still active in mind and body.*

Dada is an example of someone who requires strict structure of his day
in order to maintain his sense of well-being. Discipline defines his body;
his faith defines his soul. Although he lives in a protected environment,
he lives his life in a way that is a model to his community of how to
conduct oneself in the elder years.

SOME MEN DODGE THE BULLET

Despite, or sometimes because of, ups and downs or traumas along the
way, some men seem to continue or to move seamlessly into position as
time passes. I joined **John M.** at his office in Philadelphia, Pennsylvania;
at age sixty-six, he is treasurer and executive director of an insurance
company that has been in existence since 1769. Though of retirement age,
he has opted not to retire—at least not yet.

*I really like to work. My company served Episcopal clergy and their
families, and my involvement with the church has always been sub-
stantial. This is a full-time job, but my hours are very flexible. Because
I can set my own time and set my own schedule, I feel almost like I'm
volunteering. I'm doing something I thoroughly enjoy. I feel as though
I'm helping people. And I'm so happy that I don't have to do fund-
raising. We manage our investments well and wisely. And we do good
things for people. My contacts with clients are all by appointment. No
drop-ins. Also, because of technology, I can do my work from anywhere. It's a perfect job for me. In a sense I feel as though I'm retired
and volunteering because I can set my own schedule. If I weren't
getting paid at this, I'd want to do it as a volunteer. So, no, I don't
want to ever retire! I've been in several businesses but never had to be
at a certain place at a certain time. I've always chafed at that.*

Of course, John is in an enviable position, not available to most people. He can retire—or not—according to his own wishes. He can obviously afford to continue to work at this job that he gets so much satisfaction
from, regardless of whether he is paid. So, for John, no identity issues or

social adjustments have suddenly moved into his life. But, as we will see later, he will confront other issues at this stage in his life.

People who meet **Herbert G.** are invariably impressed by the energy, enthusiasm, and warmth they immediately encounter. He is likely to give you a strong hug and a kiss on the cheek, whatever your gender. His ninety-five years are irrelevant, even on the slower-than-they-used-to-be walks he takes in Philadelphia's famous Rittenhouse Square, across from his apartment building. The cane or walker is mainly a precaution against falling. When he recently accompanied one of the seniors he visits as a volunteer to the man's physical therapy, Herbert, who himself works with a physical trainer at the VA, says, "I showed the therapist some of my moves."

Herbert retired from endodontic dentistry (he was a pioneer root-canal specialist and an army dental surgeon in World War II) in 2005 because of macular degeneration in one eye, which impeded his ability to focus properly. His request to his shocked retinologist to destroy the vision in the affected eye so he could use only the healthy eye was denied. Even though he no longer could practice or teach, Herbert says:

> I never felt I lost my identity. I continued in a study group that started years ago with five or six of us in a professor's office. Now it is enormous. Often over one hundred people attend a meeting; we have guest speakers from around the country. A few years ago, we had a speaker from New York. I was sitting quietly in the back. At one point, he noticed me and insisted I take a bow as he told the audience I had once been his professor. That was very nice. I remain interested in what is new. So I feel that I never gave up dentistry per se, even as I could no longer practice and became involved in other activities.

LOST AND FOUND

It's easy to talk to **Ed B.** of Valley Forge, Pennsylvania, and New York, New York. He is a big man who seems younger than his eighty years, with a big youthful presence and a feisty energy that can fill the room. You sense his commitment to what he does in every word he says. Ed recognized the need for change when he was fifty-five. Now eighty, he continues to follow the path he discovered twenty-five years ago. After college and graduate school for economics and English, followed by the service, Ed began a highly successful career in sales in a small printing company that grew to national prominence. Married at twenty-six, he went through a traumatic divorce at thirty-eight when his wife left him, taking their three children halfway across the country. "You can't raise children over the telephone," he observed. He also noted wryly, "I come from an Irish family; everyone was drunk."

> *The office was like* Madmen. *We drank from 10 a.m. and went right through. We opened up a bar at 4 o'clock and entertained all the time. I traveled all over the country, and we drank. I had a wonderful time in a very competitive business. I gave up drinking at fifty, and at fifty-five I became terrified of retirement; I knew that I was getting too old for the business and would have to retire before long. I had worked all my life—since I was thirteen. I had no hobbies, didn't play golf. I found a marvelous therapist, two sessions a week for two hours, who was disabled from a serious auto accident. We talked a lot about Eastern religions, an interest we shared. I went to AA for many years, just don't have time now.*
>
> *At fifty-six I started back to school at night for four years at the New School, taking every course they had on addiction, which had caused so many problems in my life. The school said they had nothing else to offer and recommended I become an intern. I asked where I, feeling like the oldest living student, could go. I spent a year at a well-known drug and alcohol facility, working every night as a licensed drug and alcohol counselor. I loved it. I met a great psychiatrist at Bellevue Hospital and started working with her there and never left. I still go there on Mondays and Tuesdays, continuing even after she retired. When I was sixty I started thinking about how long I might live and decided it was time to learn something about death. I became a hospice volunteer for seven years, going into homes in North Philly where it was considered too dangerous to send women. I didn't know what to expect, but I absolutely loved it. No one talked about death. They wanted to live. It was the most wonderful experience of my life.*

Ed's energy surely accounts in part for his ability to pursue his new interests while winding up life in the commercial world. The partner to whom he was committed was working in New York, and the couple still resides in two places: New York and Valley Forge. When his life in sales was formally over, he was fully engaged in counseling.

What continues to motivate you?

I woke up one day about ten years ago and looked at my hand and thought, "That's pretty good." There are twenty-seven bones in the human hand. It's infinite in what it can do. I'm not responsible for the creation of that hand. Something else is. I look at nature and see that everything in nature from the smallest molecule to as big as you want to get is in service for something else. Everything—the sun, chemicals in the soil. This germ of a thought about service stayed with me.

When I was in business I went away for a week every three years to think about my job and my life. I would analyze my assets—not money. I still do this. I know my faults and my strengths, and I feel I need to use the strong points and passions I have to help other people live. Being a good counselor is in my genes—I love it, and I love the people. For seven years I worked at an AIDS hospital in New York with street people. I think every human, good or bad, deserves dignity and my respect. I never care how they treat me; I'm tough. I love to hear someone say, "I'm doing better." What else is there?

Ten years ago I decided I didn't know my neighbors in our 265-home development and also realized that they had a lot more than they needed. I went around to all of them and told them to leave one can of something out on their driveways every Sunday for me to pick up. Now, every Sunday, rain or shine or snow, I pick up groceries to the tune of anywhere from $800 to $1,000 a week. I also collect clothes and take $2,000 to $4,000 worth of clothes with me to Bellevue—Hospital, in New York—even computers sometimes. I feel privileged to do this.

When I first went to Bellevue I started the Men's Over-Fifty Club with one rule: you don't bend over to pick up anything because everything hurts. After about ten years I thought, "I'm old now." I decided to volunteer at a senior center for drop-ins. I play the piano. There are always around thirty or forty men and women. We sing old songs. Sometimes I'll call for attention and say very seriously, "Who was your first crush?" Nobody forgets that, and they love to talk about it. Many of them have had strokes. They're beautiful people with so much to give. I remember walking into the back door of a nursing home on Route 1 one time, and these poor people were sitting there focused on this TV set. When the door opened, they all turned around to see if it was someone to visit them. We can handle that; we can do it—particularly for the bedridden ones. There's a great program that's been tried

with Skyping visits for nursery homes. Unfortunately, bureaucracy al-
most always gets in the way.

But Ed keeps trying. When one program fails, or runs into a sea of red tape, he goes on to the next, if necessary. He is never without knowing he is needed and never without a feeling of fulfillment.

You will learn more about **Jim B.** in chapter 4. Retired at sixty-two after decades of corporate work as a type A executive in control of his own work and that of people who worked for him, we wondered how he copes with or has questions about his identity now that he is no longer in that role. Here is Jim's take on this issue:

Giving that up is a tough thing to face for a lot of people, but I'm okay with that. I know who I am. It's just a matter of finding what you can be passionate about, finding your satisfaction other ways, accomplishing for your other concerns. I'm not really worried about that. There's a lot that I'm passionate about. I realize that I have all this experience, and yet one day I was there and the next day I was not, but from the firm's standpoint mandatory retirement makes a lot of sense. It gives younger people an opportunity to step up and grow professionally. On the other hand, here you have all this store of knowledge and nowhere to place it. It has no value for what I'm doing now except that it gives me a transferable skill set for some of the things that I might be doing. I will start looking for some board positions, which in itself is work.

I've met many men who are depressed, bitter, angry at this stage. They didn't expect thirty more years of active, vigorous time when they can be involved in the world. They don't take the reins and do something with this gift of time. Some just go on existing and don't know what to do with their time. You must go on living, loving, learning. You must get out of your comfort zone, just like you did when you were working.

AGEISM (AGAIN)

Here we suggest you reread chapter 1. Think about ageism again and how you personally confront and fight against it. Your very existence makes you a role model for other men you don't even know. Be a good one.

THE UPSHOT

All through life, not only at retirement, "Who am I?" is a central issue. Some people go through their lives so occupied, so unreflective, that they are always too busy to know who they are. But at retirement the brakes are suddenly applied, and they are forced to shift gears. Their daily routines and interactions change and require attention. The man in the mirror may look different—not only older but also unfamiliar. Furthermore, if they never thought about it before, they are now realizing that attitudes toward the simple fact of time marching on may be presenting roadblocks they never anticipated.

Many men become angry and bitter, resentful and depressed when they confront the loss of their control, their power, and even their identity during retirement. Arthur S., Alfred Stillman, Bruce G., Govind T., John M., Ed B., and Jim B. are seven examples of men who have manned up to changing identities in retirement in their own ways. Arthur S. is floundering a bit, trying valiantly to work at keeping busy. We're confident that he'll do better, since he's aware that he needs to make some changes. Alfred Stillman is having a difficult comeuppance right now. We'll see more fully how he copes in the next two chapters. Bruce G. recognizes that a reinvention of self will be required if he is to continue his emotionally successful life. Govind T. set a strict structure for himself that gives him the self-discipline he craves to remain happy and fulfilled. John M. and Bernard G. may be among the lucky few for whom retirement and work life will be a seamless transition. Ed B. recognized what was coming and set his new course early on for a life of service he found through manning up to his own demons. Isn't that the aim of us all?

If you didn't know before, here's your chance to find out who you really are.

3

STAYING THE COURSE: LONGER, FARTHER, DEEPER

The job of the artist is always to deepen the mystery.

—Francis Bacon

RETIRE? SOME SAY "NEVER!" AND THEY MEAN IT

There are those among us who not only will not but also cannot retire from a life's work. Artists, for example, cannot, because being an artist is not a choice. It is who and what a person is, no matter the form that the art may take. It is a condition, not an occupation. Nonartists, too, discover a passion or commitment early on in life that never wavers. It may be a scientific quest or dedication to an ideal or calling that lasts beyond the mundane strictures of work schedules. The idea of seeking an alternate focus for one's concentration is not even considered, despite the suggestions or urgings of others to cultivate new interests that might displace the old.

"It's time," they're told. "Now that you're [fill in your number], it's time to widen your horizons, to do something new. Time's a-wasting!"

But these are people for whom the gift of more time affords the opportunity to delve even more deeply into what turned them on to the calling they felt in the first place. Most people don't fit into this category. The men in this chapter are probably reading this book because they are curious about other men's lives and concerns. They themselves have never escaped, or wanted to, what first ignited their imagination. Perhaps they couldn't have even if they tried. While some unplanned-for occupations developed as they had to earn a living, perhaps support a family, they did not get in the way; instead, they often advanced the inner drive in a specific direction.

These men have been on an occupational trajectory that has taken them from early days of interest or discovery to an ever-deepening commitment to knowledge or to expression of what they continue to learn. For the men you will meet in subsequent chapters, who discover a passion later in life, who reconfigure occupations or careers in newly satisfying and productive ways, or who rekindle unfulfilled dreams, or who are still seekers, the experience of the person whose life follows a clear and discernible path is fascinating. Meet them here first; you will encounter some of their thoughts again throughout the book as they, too, share thoughts and comments about relationships and life in general.

Digging Deeply: Seeking Justice

Just by luck, as we dined one night at Paloma, our favorite restaurant in Philadelphia, Barb Cohan-Saavedra (owner, with her chef husband), who is an attorney, former US prosecutor, and dessert maker extraordinaire, overheard my mention of the Vidocq Society.[1] She approached our table just as I was explaining what it is and why it piques my mystery-loving side and said, "Thelma, try this new gelato flavor I've developed. And, by the way, I'm on the board of Vidocq. Would you like to attend a meeting with me one day?"

The board meets at the Union League once a month for lunch, and I would be her guest to hear the presentation of an unsolved murder by interested parties from anywhere in the world to a group of experts who gather to listen and offer advice, which may aid in solving the crime. The experts, VSMs—Vidocq Society members—are current and former FBI profilers, homicide investigators, scientists, psychologists, prosecutors, and coroners, selected by committee invitation only. It is named for nineteenth-century French detective (and former criminal) Eugène François Vidocq, who was a pioneer in helping police solve cold-case murders. The society's three founders were a forensic sculptor from Philadelphia, a prison psychologist from Michigan, and **William S. Fleisher** (no relation to the author), who heads the society.

When I was introduced to the presiding, neatly bearded Vidocq commissioner himself after the luncheon, which was attended by a mostly male group of more than eighty VSMs, he agreed to meet one day for a conversation.

Which side of the justice system?

Now seventy-three, Bill has no intentions of retiring—ever.

I'll work 'til I drop!

His life is too full, too satisfying, too fascinating and energizing, personally and professionally. How did this happen to a failing high school student, the short, underachieving, disappointing, belligerent third child of a 6'3" handsome, prominent dentist who always found his youngest child wanting? The kid who immersed himself in comic books thought surely to be signs of "juvenile delinquency" and for whom college was definitely not in the cards? The future for the kid who was always getting in trouble on the playground, in school, or even being hauled home by police (who became his heroes) did not augur well to the family.

Here's the thread: A fascination with homicide dating to childhood fears stoked by local true stories of a neighborhood teenage murderer, the riveting poster of a dead child ("the boy in the box") that haunted young Bill and who remains unidentified to this day, the need to be tough and defend himself physically, and compassion for underdogs. And past the desire for a distant father's approval, a firm sense of good versus evil, the desire to right wrongs where he saw them, and *perhaps* a dream of knighthood. One can picture him in shining armor!

A conversation with Bill Fleisher reminds us that high school performance and predictions so often entirely miss the mark and that strong people can and usually do survive them. After two years in the army, a seriously toughening experience, Bill did go to college at Temple University, his dad's alma mater.

I studied sociology, which I loved. [Bill cited studies he still remembers for their impact.] Then I joined the Philadelphia police force. When I was a cop I was very aware of the unfairness to victims—and to witnesses of crimes. This is back before there were ombudsmen. Witnesses could be called back so many times. It was awful. I felt *nobody speaks for the dead guy who left a wife and kids. Everyone's worried about the piece of **** that killed him. Then when I was studying for the detective rank I first read about Vidocq; later I read his memoir in French when I was a federal agent. I thought, "Why doesn't anyone give this guy credit for what he did for investigation?"*

That was the start of the society, on a federal Monday when I was off and could meet with these other guys for lunch. It was so intellectually stimulating to talk about cases.

Always a cop? Digging deeper?

I joined the FBI for five years, mainly undercover work, once long-term against the mob in New York State, specializing in organized crime. I also played a chemist for a while and recovered a half-million dollars in drugs. I even was a stand-up comedian on a Caribbean cruise and arrested the crew for smuggling. My partner [in Keystone Intelligence Network] says I'm a chameleon—wherever I go, I blend in. After stints in various places and in Washington, DC, I joined US Customs to get back to Philadelphia with my wife and newborn baby. I retired as assistant special agent in charge [ASAC] of the US Customs' Office of Investigations in Philadelphia after eleven years. As a director of Keystone Intelligence I specialize in forensic interrogation and polygraph investigation. I've also done training in these areas internationally.

Bill's facility for languages, as well as his memory for jokes, serves him well:

It's all in the ear. Mostly all you need is to function at the level of a five-year-old. That's where I am in Thai and Arabic. Italian, German, French, and Spanish are much better.

"'Til I Drop!"

For Bill Fleisher, there is nothing to retire from. Moving from the police force to the FBI to Customs to Keystone did not mark retirements—merely shifts of the prism through which he views the world and his role in it. There are always wrongs to be righted, mysteries to be solved, injustices to be exposed, and there always will be. If you find him on social media, you will see that bigotry and "unfairness" in any form stirs his ire today as much as it did when he was a boy. He is a literal American flag-waver, clear in expressing his devotion to country and equally clear in expressing his dismay at anything he perceives as his country's persecution of anyone in any form. Champion of the underdog (including the four-legged variety), he expresses that vision in all he does. His energy is undiminished. He has seen much of the dark side of life but views it from the light, a perspective he resolves to maintain.

I don't think anybody any time in history has been so fortunate to live in the time I live in. I've seen the change of a millennium. Great advances in science, medicine, the arts. Wars, too. I've gotten to see so many wonderful things, but I haven't gotten to see peace on Earth. Not many people see the change of a century!

THE ACTIVIST

Jose S. of Camden, New Jersey, seventy-eight, was able to express his social consciousness and lifelong concern for the welfare of others through his professional life in social work.

My first retirement experience was when I was sixty-two. After two months, it drove me crazy, and I decided to get a job and worked for about nine months at something I didn't want to do. So I quit that job and decided I needed to leave a legacy. I'm not a wealthy man. Can't leave money. I had to volunteer and leave a footprint. So for the last fifteen years I've been working with the Senior Environment Corps. They told me that if I want to work here, I have to be a supervisor. I said, "I don't want to be a supervisor—I want to work directly with clients." So they made me a supervisor of supervisors. So I had to switch from working with the families to working with the workers. I had to help them become better workers. It's a different kind of satisfaction and a different kind of legacy, but it's there.

I also helped start a garden and nature center in my town and taught in the AARP safe-driver program. I'm a volunteer at the aquarium and serve on the board of the Hispanic Family Center. I need to be busy!

What Jose does is not "busywork." Each activity has great meaning for him—and for others.

Recently I was on a bus to Trenton to speak to our representatives about climate change, and I was so happy to see that about 15 percent were senior citizens. I think it's important for us seniors to have a presence in advocacy groups. I go to many demonstrations, and I carry my signs and I shout. Lots of seniors were there from the sixties because that's how we were raised. That's what we did. That's what was expected. What's different now is we're beginning to think how we can carry on the cause beyond our own lives. We're not always going to be able to walk that line.

I believe in young people and what they can achieve, and I know their challenges are every bit as difficult as ours were in the sixties. More, even. They have to know they're not alone. We are needed more than ever. We can't keep going two steps forward, three steps back in social progress.

I see the other side. I maintain a membership in a suburban Rotary Club, whose members are very conservative. I need to hear them, too. I know there's a bigger world. Climate change doesn't exist as an issue in the Rotary Club. Democracy is a chaotic process, but avoiding the chaos doesn't help anything.

Jose definitely is never bored. And his mind is still wide open. Encouraging? Inspiring, perhaps?

THE MUSIC NEVER STOPS

Oscar, an opera based on the life and writings of Oscar Wilde, had its world premiere at the Santa Fe Opera in 2013 and the premiere of the revised version in Philadelphia in 2015. The music is by **Theodore Morrison** and the libretto by Morrison and English opera director John Cox. How does a first opera happen when the composer is in his mid-seventies? Did Morrison always write music? No—it turns out that composing started at forty. Talking with Theo was revelatory. In hindsight, the opera had to happen; Theo's music never stops.

Theo still lives and works in Ann Arbor, Michigan, where he retired in 2005 from the University of Michigan School of Music as director of graduate studies in conducting and directed the choirs as a member of the faculty for nearly twenty years. His compositions have been performed throughout North America and Europe and in Asia, Australia, New Zealand, and, recently, Cuba.

We asked where Theo had gone to school to prepare for a career. The future distinguished director of choirs and conductor of the chamber orchestra at the Peabody Conservatory of Music of the Johns Hopkins University and faculty member at Smith College and at Michigan never went to college himself.

When did you know?

My earliest musical memory was going to hear Peter and the Wolf *when I was about six years old. Later, I was playing with some kids in an alley behind our house in Baltimore and picked up a stick and started thrashing it around, pretending I was a conductor. The other kids made fun of me when I told them I was going to be a conductor. In elementary school we had a terrible piano class with cardboard keyboards on our desks and one real piano where the teacher had us take turns. The teacher told my mother that I had "unpianistic" fingers and probably shouldn't go on with music, but my mother didn't believe her and sent me to a teacher outside. I began to play much better and fell in love with music.*

How did you learn?

When I was fourteen I sang in a church choir. My choirmaster had seen some talent in me and suggested organ lessons. He introduced me to the organ music of Bach. That was moving and exciting and changed my life. By the time I was nineteen I was offered a full-time job as organist-choirmaster at the Cathedral of the Incarnation in Baltimore after my predecessor was drafted in the army. So I guess I learned by doing. I've always been a voracious reader, so you could say I'm largely "self-taught" in the sense that my only long-term mentors were my keyboard teachers. For conducting, I used to hang around Baltimore Symphony rehearsals, and the conductor, Sergiu Comissiona, would let me sit behind the orchestra to observe. I learned by asking the musicians questions and by listening to the changes in the sound that developed as a result of Mr. Comissiona's terrific work. Conducting great music has taught me composition. Preparing all that music for performance tells you what works and what doesn't.

As for my own music, European papers have referred to me as "the American composer, Theodore Morrison," but, as far as I'm concerned, I'm just Theo, the composer, more influenced by European musicians than by Americans. I think in later years I've become influenced to some extent by modern pop culture and jazz. I'm proud of my son's work as a rock musician. While I have almost no understanding of it, I find it exciting and intellectually stimulating to see how he works; he's had a profound effect on my respect for certain aspects of popular culture.

Have you ever retired?

When I had my official retirement from the University of Michigan, I said, "I quit"—not in anger, just that I was announcing that I was moving on to other things. I learn so much from the new things I do. Writing for opera—as for theater—requires working with a team, even learning to consign to the cutting-room floor pages of my own music I loved and now no longer remember. Being able to make changes on the eve of a performance!

In a succession of careers within music, Theo has, as all artists and performers do, had to risk failure or criticism often.

If I can look at my own life as a total and say with Kipling, "I've met with Triumph and Disaster and treated those two imposters just the same," maybe when the time comes I'll be able to leave this earth a happy man. I'm fortunate to live a long life of seventy-eight years and expect to live longer. Life is better at this stage. My body certainly doesn't work as well, but my mind does, and my heart is more open than it ever has been.

HAVE MICROSCOPE, WILL EXAMINE

Irving R. of Sarasota, Florida, is a remarkable centenarian of boundless energy, charm, and dynamism. That's right—he is one hundred years old. I asked what he did before he retired and how he felt about retirement when he approached it. Irving had led a life of enormous activity and involvement in the New York City school system. It turned out that Irving may have been retired in the sense that careers ended, but through them all he was what he still is—a scientist. Before this conversation, I attended a wonderful lecture Irving gave about Einstein.

I've worn many caps. At the time I retired, I was chairman of the science department at a high school in Brooklyn, New York, coauthored books, worked for the College Board, wrote examinations for the Board of Examiners for teacher licensing. They wanted me to be an administrative assistant, which I reluctantly accepted for one term. I hate administration. It takes me away from what I like to do. I love science and I love teaching and didn't want to leave science. My program was a biomedical program which crossed district lines. For over thirty years I was adjunct professor of biology at CCNY with the understanding that if I completed my doctorate, there would be a position waiting for me. I did all my studies. However, World War II came along. I joined the military. I wanted to fight Hitler. When I came back four years later I was married and we wanted to have a family, so I never completed my PhD—which is one of the great sorrows of my life. But I had a busy life nevertheless. I was involved in writing several books, worked for several national foundations and committees, several of which continued after my retirement.

Actually, I was very, very worried about my approaching retirement because I never had had fewer than three or four jobs concurrently: I taught in high school, taught in college, coauthored books, worked for the College Board, wrote examinations for the Board of Examiners to teacher licensing.

My friends were older and had preceded me in retirement, and they took me under their wing. It helped to see my friends as role models in retirement, and I saw that they were happy. They were a very intellectually stimulating group of people who had been major players in the education world in New York. We formed a group and decided to make a survey of all the microorganisms around Long Island. We were just a group of friends who went around collecting fresh-water, salt-water, and brackish-water specimens. We continued to pursue our curiosity in basic biology, with no thought of monetary gain or professional fame. We also went to theater, ballet, and tracked birds. So this was my transition to retirement—with the help of my friends. My wife also worked and did voluntary work. Her artwork filled our home.

I had no identity problem when I retired. I continued being a biologist. I have been an extremely fortunate person. The only misfortune is that in living so long I have lost so many people.

The pile of magazines and books on Irving's desk is testimony to his enduring interest in science. Before I left, he took me to the small balcony in his apartment where he cultivates unusual plants. Irving pursues all of his interests despite severe hearing and vision problems. But more about how he copes with his disabilities later.

ONE HUNDRED PLAYS AND COUNTING

Fame has never been the goal for playwright **Walt Vail** of Pitman, New Jersey. At eighty-eight, he continues to write, lead a playwriting group, and submit and see new plays produced in a variety of venues, including off-Broadway in New York at the Open Eye Theater, which is now based in Margaretville, New York. One of his latest, *La Duse: Woman & Actor*, won a playwriting contest in Beverly, Massachusetts, and was performed there recently. A new play about theater, *Tybalt & Mercutio Live!*, played in a small theater in New York in 2015. And *Young Frederick Douglass*, about the slave who became one of America's most famous abolitionists, premiered at a church in Philadelphia in 2016.

I have known Walt for more than twenty-five years, since he was a pivotal figure when we started Philadelphia Young Playwrights. His quiet, kindly demeanor always conveyed both acceptance of others' voices and authority as he led workshops for teachers and playwrights who then would be working with schoolchildren of all ages. It was impossible to sit in on one of his workshops and not write, even if you had never attempted a scene before.

We talked over coffee in my kitchen.

I put together a play last year called Case & Trial for John Peter Zenger—*had an excellent reading of it. It took a lot of research and work. I discovered the dictum "write what you know" doesn't work for me. I want to learn about what I don't know. In recent years I fell in love with Eleanora Duse, the great Italian actress; she was so fascinating. I realized she was an abused woman. I started to write about her several years ago, then thought maybe it wasn't for me and put the play aside. When I picked it up last year, I saw that she was a transitional figure in theater. Chekhov saw her! Shaw wrote about her! Her naturalistic acting changed things. When I worked in schools, I'd think about a play all year and write it in the summer.*

Unlike the many children whose lives Walt has reached, both directly and through their teachers, he never heard of or knew about playwriting as a child or teenager.

My family was very poor. My stepfather made fifteen dollars a week. My mother had five children when I was young, eventually six altogether. All four brothers slept together in two bunk beds, mother in another room with the girls, and my stepfather in his own room. My mother left the farm in central Pennsylvania with a girlfriend at sixteen for Philadelphia and got tangled with two of the most dysfunctional men imaginable! The welfare department got me a four-hour-a-day job at the GE plant. I had to go from school and got out at eight o'clock. I quickly learned that I never wanted to spend my life in a factory job.

How did you learn?

I was a mediocre student in the mechanical arts course in high school. I actually spent my whole high school career in the library, reading. But I saw that some of my classmates were going to college and realized I had enough credits to do that, so I worked all summer loading boxcars for the railroad, earned $300, enough for tuition, jumped on a train—literally—with a friend and went to State College, Pennsylvania, with no place to stay! Penn State was welcoming veterans and had an area filled with cots for them. I got one, and the veterans told me to go into the service and get the GI Bill—and that was the answer. I've been a Truman Democrat ever since. In fact, I'm researching Truman right now for a play about his dropping the bombs. He had many regrets about those bombs.

The Coast Guard had a two-year enlistment. My friend and I went in, which gave me three and a half years of college, and I was anxious to get back. Semesters were only four to five months long. At Penn State I took a course in playwriting from a playwright who became a surrogate father for me. He didn't mean to, but I had no good father figure growing up. A social worker in Philadelphia who was my age ran a theater group for her agency and read some of the plays I sent from Penn State. After Penn State I came to Philadelphia, and we even acted together in some of the plays she put on.

And what might we learn?

A long life devoted to expression through an art that requires sensitivity to human relationships and development, to knowledge of oneself and others, to seeing life through others' (characters') eyes and hearts, could provide some hints to living for the rest of us. Walt has lots to tell us in other aspects of doing well as a new senior man and making the most of a longer life's challenges and opportunities. You will meet him again in subsequent chapters.

REINVENTION WAS THE KEY

More than twenty years ago, before he returned to the "classical role of the physician,"[2] **Alfred Stillman**, MD, wrote an article that was published in the prestigious *New England Journal of Medicine*.[3] He was still in his fifties then. The article was an eye-opener for many at the time. Like many precocious students sure of their interest from an early age, and encouraged by supportive, proud parents who had great faith in his future, Alfred excelled in high school, college, and medical school in New York. At the time Alfred first became a physician, he, his parents, and his wife, Paula, who also graduated from medical school and worked in administrative positions, viewed being a doctor as difficult, to be sure, but definitely secure, as well as noble and rewarding. "Losing one's job" was not in the cards for physicians, as it often was in most other professions. Alfred and Paula certainly did not foresee years of professional changes and times of insecurity.

When the journal article appeared in print, Alfred had been a gastroenterologist briefly in Norfolk, Virginia. Previously he and Paula had lived for thirteen years in Tucson, Arizona, where the number of specialists had grown far beyond the population's needs. Alfred could see changes coming, but his own practice flourished. They moved, however, to Worcester, Massachusetts, when Paula was offered a position as associate dean at a medical school there. As Alfred and Paula adjusted to the vagaries of their two careers, he published numerous articles while in private practice and served as a hospital's chief of internal medicine. Before long, another move, to Norfolk, Virginia, presented what seemed to be a great opportunity for Paula. The move to Norfolk was brief; Paula became dean of a medical school, and Alfred had been offered a position in his specialty on the medical school staff. Within a few months of the move, however, both positions were lost.

Alfred and I talked in the Stillmans' beautiful condo in Philadelphia, where they moved because the number of hospitals and universities in the city afforded new possibilities. We were surrounded by impressive sculpture and other artwork, artifacts of world travel and their appreciation of other cultures. How has "reinvention" been his key to a life still dedicated to medicine, intellectual curiosity and stimulation, and personal satisfaction? How has he emerged from depression (you'll be meeting Alfred again on this topic) to a healthy view of his life today?

My advice to anyone contemplating retirement? Don't do it. If you don't like what you do, reinvent yourself. It's never too late. When we came to Philadelphia, after a long, fruitless search for [gastroenterology] jobs, I took a fellowship in geriatrics. I knew that the elderly were the fastest-growing segment of the population in the country but that American fellowships produced only one hundred new geriatricians each year. I was older than all of my teachers. Some of them could not stop calling me "Dr. Stillman" while they called all the other fellows by their first names.

I have always loved talking to and getting to know people. I found that I especially enjoyed doing home visits for elderly patients who were unable to leave their homes. When I visit an elderly patient, I love learning about that person. Sometimes I can get to know really important things just by poking around in the kitchen, seeing what is in the cupboard and refrigerator.

Alfred's reinvention as a geriatrician has expanded to his dedication to the classic model of the physician we knew as children—the one who comes to your home. In his practice he includes not only the elderly but also others "who are unable to get to a doctor's office and the doctor can't or won't come to them." He gets to know, appreciate, and love his patients and their caregivers individually as the heroic examples they are. He dedicates his book, *Home Visits: A Return to the Classical Role of the Physician*, to his family and concludes the dedication "to my patients, both living and dead, who have always reminded me why I love my profession."

ONLY THE TITLES HAVE CHANGED

Robert G. of Chicago, Illinois, is another example of a man who, though retired, has maintained a strong connection to the lifestyle and goals of his preretirement days. The forces that drove him then drive him still. We often see the man who was chairman of the board in his businesses, large or small, who remains chairman of the board of the charity he promotes, and who became chairman of the board of the condo he lives in. Bob seems to be one of these men. He always took on positions of leadership and control and still continues to do so. These are men who succeeded under pressure and thrived in a competitive world. They often seek out similar roles in retirement.

> *I have been a widower for seven years. I was a partner in a major law firm in Chicago and then went to a client as principal counsel and practiced there until two years ago. I'm now eighty-six, and I've only recently retired. I've lived in Chicago all my life except for my time in the army and when I was a student at the University of Illinois.*

Did you experience an identity change when you retired? How do you feel about this recent transition?

> *Well, I would have continued working until my client went out of business. But, no, I didn't feel any change in identity when I left my law firm. Maybe that's because I never really retired. Actually, people still request my advice on many things. At the time I found I have other interests besides being a lawyer. I'm captain of patrol boys in an elementary school. I'm always captain of something: president of old peoples' homes, board member and president of many Jewish organizations, director of the Department of Politics at Brandeis University for the past fifty years, active in politics in the city of Chicago. I was instrumental in electing Harold Washington, the first black mayor of Chicago. I was a founding member of the alderman's assembly. I'm now no longer so active in politics. I've passed the mantle to a younger group.*

You can see by Robert's postretirement activities that he has maintained his interest in control and leadership of the undertakings and responsibilities that he seeks. He has always been a take-charge kind of guy and continues to be one. In this sense, retirement didn't change who he is.

Indeed, he reports that he has felt no loss of identity during his retirement years.

SEEKING—AND FINDING—ONENESS

In the one-room schoolhouse in Broken Bow, Nebraska, in 1945, five-year-old **Roger D. Nelson** could not possibly imagine that life would ever take him as far as it has in so many ways. In nearby North Platte, the high-school Bausch + Lomb Award and a scholarship to the University of Rochester took him away from Nebraska and then on to Princeton, New Jersey, where he and his wife eventually made their home more than thirty-five years ago. In his early postcollege days, Roger seemed to be taking Yogi Berra's advice as forks appeared in the road. One led to a long successful marriage when he was serving overseas in military intelligence in the army and met the local (German) woman in charge of the PX. Back in New York City, six months later, he realized what was missing, called her, and proposed, and she accepted. Out of the army, he joined the protest against the Vietnam War, in which he had lost friends. At NYU he took part in the takeover of a building during the protest days.

In retrospect, it was not surprising that we had met Roger at an annual meditation retreat in the Catskills to which we were invited after appearing on Sister Jenna's *America Meditating Radio Show* to talk about our book *The New Senior Woman*. By definition, a meditation retreat provides an experience of shared consciousness, and that, we eventually learned, is of particular interest to Roger. We learned much more about that later when we met for coffee and a leisurely chat in Princeton several months later.

Training, experience, intellectual curiosity, and his self-description as "spiritual, not formally religious" led Roger to his life's work, which enabled him to draw upon his background in experimental psychology and psychophysiology, physics, statistical methods, engineering, and multimedia production. After teaching psychology at Johnson State College in northern Vermont, he worked for more than twenty years as coordinator of research at the Princeton Engineering Anomalies Research laboratory at Princeton University.

Was that retirement time?

No. It overlapped with my becoming director of the Global Conscious-ness Project [GCP], which I still direct from my home office. Collective Consciousness remains my focus.

Author's Note: For the statistically sophisticated, we recommend Goo-gling Roger D. Nelson or Global Consciousness Project or watching his YouTube hour lecture describing the GCP. There you will find descrip-tions and explanations of the scientific bases for Roger's research.

For the rest of us, a much simpler picture emerges: From everything Roger has learned and continues to pursue through science and the use of random-number generators in a worldwide network of collaborating sci-entists and engineers he formed, he seeks and has found evidence of human interconnectedness (collective consciousness) at various signifi-cant times, times when, according to him, "we are bound together in a synchrony of thinking and feeling."

Surely, finding such evidence is unlikely to be completed in our life-time. But its pursuit, which suggests proof of a relationship among hu-mans beyond the physical and nonphysical, and the possibilities for good in cooperative intention on the part of humanity, is worthy of a lifetime's dedication. It receives this dedication on the part of a man whose idea of legacy is "just trying to make things better," who expresses sadness that "people don't even realize that they—innocently—teach their prejudices to vulnerable children," and who refers to the Dalai Lama's teaching that the practice of compassion affects both the individual and society.

Today's world requires something new. Humans are, I believe, con-nected at a deep level. That consciousness can be either negative or positive. It's time to accept oneness as modern wisdom.

Roger quotes a Navajo poem that says:

When you put a thing in order
And you are all in accord
And you give it a name
Then it becomes.

HOW ABOUT YOU?

Is this what you've done? Followed a course that started when you were young and seen it change and be a source of fulfillment continually? Or has a passion remained steady even as it has sometimes changed shape with the demands of life, always remaining the core of what you do and who you are, maturing in its expression even as you do? If that's the case, we hope you give some time to counting your blessings.

4

NEW PATHS

When you see a fork in the road, take it.

—Yogi Berra

Apparently Yogi Berra really did say this. He explained that originally he was giving a visitor driving directions to his home and never imagined it would become the advice for living and decision making that it has for so many people. We laugh at one of his famous Yogi-isms, but in this time of unexpected longevity, more men see the fork in the road than ever before. You are part of the Longevity Revolution, and there is plenty of science to back it up. No longer is there a clear, if bumpy, path from childhood and youth to work life, to a fairly short period of retirement or "old age." More and more four-generation families are not unusual, and a "fourth generation" is part of society, not up in the attic or out on the porch to be brought out on special occasions.

Average life expectancy in developed countries was extended by reducing infant mortality and early death until the 1970s. Since then, it has changed due to medicine's increasing ability to extend life over sixty-five; more people than ever live into their eighties, nineties, and past one hundred. By 1980 the percentage of Americans who have the possibility of reaching ninety had risen 24 percent. And while these years may not be free of chronic illnesses, most are increasingly manageable, enabling people to live autonomously and take advantage of time never afforded to past generations. Today's seventy-five-year-olds are literally as healthy as sixty-five-year-olds were fifty years ago. Every day we read of new discoveries, treatments, and even cures that turn once-fatal diseases into chronic conditions that allow for greatly extended physically active lives. Can't wait for the Australian answer to cartilage degeneration via our own stem cells to make hip and knee replacements rarities!

While society adjusts its thinking and attitudes to accommodate this Longevity Revolution, individuals can move ahead to change course completely. (Does this mean you?) Some return to a childhood or adolescent dream never fulfilled; some find a new interest to explore; some reinvent themselves. We met some men who have taken the fork and followed it.

OUT OF THE WOOD(S) AND BACK AGAIN

After retiring at sixty-two, this is how **Alan G.**, of Chappaqua, New York, describes his life five years later:

Retirement has been great—a wonderful time of life.

Did you plan it this way?

If you had told me when I was carrying cabinets up a flight of stairs to install in somebody's apartment that a few years later I would be a senior executive in an information-technology business, I would have said you were a lunatic. When I started in that field I was looking for a job, and programmers had jobs. The experience I had there kind of left me with the feeling that if you decide you want to do something, you can probably do it. You had to study and focus and work hard and all of that, but things are not out of reach. They're in reach as long as you're motivated.

When I got out of college I had no idea what I wanted to do. I got a job that was going to teach me computer programming at AT&T. I hated it—the transition from college life to this incredibly straight-laced place. I quit the job after not that long.

We were renting a little farmhouse with friends, and there were no cabinets in the kitchen. The landlord said he had boards in his shed and "you're welcome to use them if you want to make something." I borrowed an electric jigsaw from my father and figured, "How hard could this be?" I had no idea what I was doing but managed to make something that wasn't very good, but I thought it was interesting. I

*went out and knocked on cabinetmakers' doors until I got a few differ-
ent jobs and finally found a guy I worked well with and did that for five
or six years. Then I had a back injury. When you work in a cabinet
shop and you get sick, you don't get paid. It's by the hour. So I needed
to do something. I was an adult. I was married. I felt terrible that I
wasn't contributing financially. I was serious in a way I'd never been
before.*

*My alma mater had a three-day career-discovery workshop run by
grad students. I took it and came out in 1976 with recommendations
that I should be an astronomer, meteorologist, or computer program-
mer. I opened the newspaper, and there were no jobs for astronomers
or meteorologists and about five hundred for computer programmers.
I took a night class at Rutgers in the summer and found I had a knack
for it. I took a second one at night. Both teachers were very encouraging. One of them wrote me a support letter, and I went back to the
computer-sciences department, which hadn't even existed when I was
an undergraduate six or seven years earlier. One of the professors
said, "Are you sure you want to give up cabinetmaking?" Despite his
initial reaction [to my request to matriculate], he and a couple of other
professors helped structure a curriculum for me.*

After a year of taking all undergraduate courses in computer science
and relevant math, which had been his best subject in what Alan describes
as an average public-school experience, and some graduate-level courses
as well, an interview followed at Bell Labs, where he worked for one year
before beginning his thirty-two-and-a-half-year career at another major
information-technology company. Completing his master's degree was
done at night. Eventually Alan became vice president of strategy and
operations in the research department, never earning the PhD that just
about everyone else he worked with had. By the time he retired, he had
sixteen technology patents. As in most companies, the intellectual property belongs to the company, but the developer is well rewarded financially,
enabling his retirement at a young age.

Did you have anything in mind? More patents, for example?

*I had vague plans. When my wife retired eight years earlier she en-
couraged me to retire as well. At the time we talked about how much
fun we could have together and the things we could do, but I just felt
my career was going well, and I just wasn't ready. I had always liked*

athletics and knew I wanted to spend more time doing that. And I knew I wanted more time to do woodworking again. I had always kept my equipment and always insisted there be some place for it. In my career, like most executives, it was a seventy- or eighty-hour workweek with a good percentage of the time traveling, so the amount of actual time over all those decades I did woodworking was very little.

I started wood turning. I made some friends [through it], and I have a wood-turning club and a woodworking club that I go to. Once you have the time and you have interests you can have the types of relationships that weren't possible when you were working. I've taken both wood-turning and woodworking classes. I go to conferences, which I really enjoy. We have a lot of bowls. We don't know where to put them, but I enjoy making them. I've given some away to friends; I'm not sure that anything I have is valuable enough to give to charities. Also a friend put me in contact with a guy who had taken it upon himself to hire a sawyer to chop up the three hundred-year-old tree that had to come down at our synagogue. The rabbi felt that since it had been there so long something should be done with it. The sawyer chopped it into boards and brought it to a place to have the wood dried. I got involved and made a stand for the Torah out of it. The guy who hired the sawyer and I have become very close friends.

It's apparent that Alan's early love of working with wood never left. If you were to ask him his occupation today, he'd most likely say he's a wood turner, not a patent developer or researcher in technology. Not that his interest in that intellectual pursuit has left him:

When I was in research, the vast majority of the senior people were PhDs in physics. I had engineering physics as an undergraduate, but I was not at that level. When I retired I found a marvelous online physics class taught by Brian Greene, one of the top physicists. Greene has this World Science University, which is free, and the World Science Festival. When he has festivals, he has lectures, which do cost. They are fantastic. I spend a day in the city hearing lectures from top people in the field. I'm scheduled to go to one I'm very excited about because it's going to be all about Einstein. The class that I took was on relativity, so it will be a great follow-up to that.

Alan's return to his early satisfaction in working with wood gives a solid focus to this phase of life. He also "always liked athletics and wanted to spend more time doing that." He'll tell us more about that in another chapter. Stay tuned.

THE BEST OF ALL POSSIBLE WORLDS ...
FOR ONE MAN

As we say in chapter 7 about intimacy, there is no "one size fits all." **Charles D.**, of Denver, Colorado, says he can't believe he is seventy-eight. Widowed in his forties, he's been together with his second wife, Joan, for twenty-nine years and married for twenty-four of them. He says that his wife has done a spectacular job of making a family comprising his two daughters, his stepdaughter and stepson, and his three grandchildren and two stepgrandchildren "a beautifully integrated unit—a nice group." There is no doubt that Charles is one of the lucky ones in many ways. He is healthy, has a wonderful family, and is financially well off. He certainly could be living a very easy, laid-back life in retirement. He has a great deal to tell us, especially if we read between the lines and look for the ideas and attitudes that can be applicable to any life.

Still working?

I work as an investment advisor in a large financial firm. I have an arrangement with this firm that when a junior director shows up one day and they ask for Mr. D. that is my official day of retirement. I'm a numbers guy, and I figured out that if you take sleeping out of the equation, there's about 105 waking hours in a week. I work thirty hours a week, which means that I spend about 30 percent of my time working, which means I'm 70 percent retired. I decided not to retire for a bunch of reasons. At the age of sixty-nine I liquidated a business I had been in for more than forty years. It seemed to be time to do that because of the complexity of the business [manufacturing in India, importing from China] and neither daughter was interested in taking it over. I didn't see this as a time of retirement, though. It was "Where do I go from here?"

How did you find work?

The process by which I transitioned was taking the language of what I was doing specifically and bringing it into a concept level that used different but transferable skills. In other words, I took my talents and redirected them. Retail—the thrust of my business—was a balance between sales and inventory; what I'm doing in investment is a balance between hours and various sectors of the market. You just think about it more broadly.

I looked in the classified section and found five jobs that looked interesting and put together the first résumé I've ever done in my life, because I never had worked for anybody. I gave it to a neighbor who said I was skirting the issue of age. So I put in "mature judgment." I got five interviews and five offers, which I thought was amazing at the age of sixty-nine. I was kind of an experiment in the firm that I went with. They had bad experiences with kids out of college—an 80 percent dropout rate—and counted on my maturity. I became their poster boy. Good timing, work ethic, not just considering the function of what you are doing or can do out of the specific situation and considering the global or abstract picture. Look at the problem, and elevate it to the big picture.

They wanted to know why I thought I could work for someone else since I had always only worked for myself. I told them I was their best bet because I knew what it was like to be management. I asked why they would give a bunch of money to a twenty-four-year-old who was green rather than to me, who had just given up a successful business. I understand the needs, the goals, and how to get there.

What is it like being the oldest person there?

Like everywhere else. Almost everyone I know is younger than me. Nine-five percent of the seventy people at work. I'm very close to my grandchildren. I talk with them, not at them—it's not me telling them. I come down to an eye-to-eye relationship in areas we can both understand. My daughter is in academia in the area of politics and culture, and we're always talking about that. Sometimes we argue; sometimes we agree. It's always stimulating for me.

What is it about "retirement" that turns you off?

I don't say this to people because what I feel is kind of insulting—but retirement to me seems like a purgatory awaiting death. A phase between career and death. It's all about crossword puzzles, ROMEO [Retired Old Men Eating Out] lunches, and my retired friends are boring. When I'm at work, I'm involved with vital people who are doing things. Maybe my friends should read your book! The big opiate for them is classes. That's how most of them seem to be involved—and their crossword puzzles. When I think of friends and my conversations with them I find that I'm bored with conversations about which team is winning or stats about players which don't impact my life in any way. I do enjoy conversations about people's relationships in various capacities of their lives—the psychodynamics of human behavior. These discussions may impact lives in ways that may change tomorrow's actions. That to me is an exciting way to spend my time as opposed to forcing myself to do something that is time-consuming rather than thought-consuming.

I'm doing all the things I would be doing if I were retired. You asked how I spend the day. I go out. I go to movies. I belong to a movie group. I have several theater subscriptions, plus a piano and a symphony series. And I do classes at two universities. Right now I'm in the third semester of a class on the thirty-two works of Philip Roth. Marvelous class, and there's the reading for the class. The kids and grandkids take up an incredible part of my life. Not a day goes by that I'm not talking to a kid.

Some of my friends spend so much of their time going over their Medicare stuff and waiting for the mailman to come with the next bill. I'm looking forward to your book to see what else I can do when I retire. My memory is very strong. The stock market is a hobby, so I'm really working at my hobby.

How do you feel about the changes in the world today?

Well, they're not that different. They differ in the subject matter, but life is a continuum of crises and changes—from sexuality, to Title IX changes, to technology, which can bite you if you're not careful. What's going to happen when your robot outthinks you? We've always had to deal with cultural changes. Change is what's exciting about life.

Any regrets?

Of course. I'm not fifty-four. I can't write like Philip Roth. I don't understand chaos theory. I don't want to die.

Charles gives us a lot to think about. He is certainly a most fortunate man, but, as we suggested, reading between the lines provides many clues to his good luck that are more widely available than many people realize. There is no price tag on

- *intergenerational relationships.* He doesn't pander or judge but is open to their world and interest and what is different from the way we looked at the world when we were their age, and he finds common ground.
- *taking the next step.* Some people are terrified when their career is over and remain stagnant. He took age bias on and won.
- *engaging with the world.* Unlike many of his contemporaries, he is not willing to wrap himself in Saran Wrap to protect himself from the world as it changes. An ability to challenge his comfort zone may be his most salient advantage.

He also has a sense of humor.

A DIFFERENT KIND OF WOOD(S)

For **Jim B.**, sixty-two, of Philadelphia, Pennsylvania, the woods are golf clubs. But there is much, much more.

Have you noticed any difference between the way women and men approach retirement—or this stage of their lives?

> *I haven't thought about it. I worry about my own. The realm that I live in is business, management, services, executives—all those people that are "A" types, concerned about careers. Some look forward to it, and some don't. It depends on what you have outside of your professional life. I have so much outside my professional life that I couldn't do, didn't have time to do. I retired seven months ago, and now I don't have time for all the things I want to do.*

Did you have any misgivings about retiring so early?

> *A lot of people retire and want to travel the world. My wife and I have already done that. I worked overseas for thirteen years. During those years we traveled all over Europe, Africa, and the Middle East, so I*

don't have that yen to get on a plane like my friends do. That's what I did for a living—I got on a plane! It was a very exciting life. It's sometimes hard to explain that life to people who haven't lived it. I lived in Russia when everything in people's lives was managed by the state: what you ate, who you were, where you went to school. Then Russia became an open society. We lived through that transition, and it was an incredible period of time. Deciding to go that route was a big risk. But it worked out, and we grew as individuals. We developed a global view versus having a parochial view of the world.

I worked for a partnership, and we had mandatory retirement at sixty-two, so it wasn't a question of when. I could have taken early retirement, in my fifties, but I didn't consider it because I'm physically fit, mentally alert, and have lots of experience. If retirement weren't mandatory, I could have kept on working longer easily, on the one hand. But on the other hand, I could do during my sixties the thing I want to do. I figure that I can do in my sixties the things I want to do because when you start to slow down you can't always do what you want to do. You can't travel, you can't hike, play golf. I may have diminished mobility.

Do you ever think how many years you have before that will happen?

I figure that will happen in the mid-seventies. The body just wears down. I'm making sure I exercise and lead a healthy life as part of my daily routine because everything else builds from that.

What is your day like now?

I started out loving that I could do anything I wanted whenever I wanted, and after about six months I realized there was too much randomness. I felt a lack of accomplishment and realized I need more structure because I still have goals in life and things I want to do. So now I make a weekly schedule with things I want to accomplish for the week and then make sure I do it. It was so easy to put things off. As Mark Twain said, "Don't put off 'til tomorrow what you can put off 'til the day after tomorrow." I was letting too many things distract me. So far I like this method. It works for me. I had my guitar lesson, my guitar practice, my Spanish training, and my studies to become a volunteer golf-rules official. I'll do the advanced school this winter.

What is that?

I've been a golfer all my life, and I decided it would be interesting to become a golf-rules official. So how do you do that? I had to go to the US Professional [Golfers'] Association of America's rules school, then take an exam the like of which I hadn't taken for thirty-five years. I did well enough to become a volunteer for the Greater Philadelphia Golf Association. I was a rules official for eight tournaments. I did well enough in the exam to be invited to attend the advanced school this winter, so I'm preparing for that.

CREATING A WORLD

Today some people call it the "Oregon Wine Country," home as it is to more than twenty-three thousand acres of vineyards and more than five hundred wineries. It's that region in the Pacific Northwest where the Willamette River flows surrounded by mountains on three sides. No wonder so many wagon trains of immigrants made the difficult journey along the Oregon Trail in the nineteenth century to a promised land of milk and honey. Now 70 percent of the state's population live there, mostly in Portland or in Salem, the state capital. A fictional place is there, too, in the mind of one of its longtime citizens.

It is only ten miles from Salem, Oregon, where he was born eighty years ago, to Aumsville, Oregon, in the Willamette Valley, where **Gil Stewart** still lives with his wife, Roma. He and Roma met at Linfield College in Oregon and have been together ever since. Their four children and their grandchildren are all in the Northwest, not too far away. We met Gil the twenty-first-century way: via the Internet when he expressed an interest in what the ElderChicks were writing about, and we began an acquaintance by phone and e-mail. If you Google Gil, you will find not only his blog, *October Years & November Too*, but also the fictional senior world he has created, filled with people in their "October Years," as Gil calls them. (He acknowledges that by the time you read this he will have edged over into November.)

After twenty years in the family's window-manufacturing business, Gil became the business manager and administrator for his local school district, where he had served on the board. Apparently, always in the background was the young Gil who loved to write and thought of creating fiction.

> *I retired in 1998. For the next six or seven years I flailed around, not knowing where I wanted to go. I actually titled one of my blog posts "If Retirement Is So Easy, Why Did I Nearly Flunk It?" Finally in 2005 I returned to a much earlier interest in writing. Actually, I stumbled onto a forty-year-old manuscript I had stashed in the back of a closet. I didn't know it at the time, but that was my salvation.*

Fourteen Novel-Length Stories Later . . .

Not finding a publisher did not stop Gil Stewart. Despite rejections from publishing houses for his stories of senior life, his Tanner Chronicles "made [its] way into the world of ebooks and paperbacks" via Amazon.

> *Those professional judgments have not dampened my enthusiasm for telling the stories I want to tell or my attachment to the persons I have imagined into being. For those of us who write fiction, no matter what we write or how well, the stories and the persons we create take on lives of their own. We birth and nurture those individuals—the ones who inhabit our tales. We spend months, sometimes years, doing our best to bring them to life. By the story's end, those products of our imagination have become very real to us. Like all our close friends, we care about what becomes of them.*

What are the stories about?

Through his fictional characters, Gil has been able to explore the challenges and opportunities that come with the changes aging can bring. When we talked about the topics in this series, Gil said:

> *I've written about each of these subjects—sometimes whole books at a time in the Tanner Chronicles. In both the stories I began telling after retirement and the blog I write on a continuing basis I have focused on the possibilities of "thriving in our sixties and seventies." It has become something of an obsession, illustrating the many ways we can continue to "become" in late life. To the extent I am able to make that point I consider it a legacy to my readers. Beyond that, I hope to provide a positive model for our own family. What better legacy could*

*I leave than an inherited understanding that retirement does not mark
the end of becoming whatever it is we are meant to be?*

*What I call the October Years are not for sissies. Fortunately, they can
also be a time of unexpected possibilities, worthy of the best planning
we can muster. The limiting constraints of employment have been
lifted, [bringing] with it a sense of freedom we had scarcely dared to
dream about. It seems as though we have all the time in the world. But
what to do with that time? These days, twenty, even thirty years of
retirement is not uncommon. We may nurse visions of long and boring
days of sameness. Yet, if you consider the many ways your lifestyle will
change as you age, you can understand the need to be nimble and
adaptable—even in old age.*

*In today's late-life world retirement lasts longer than ever before—
because we retirees last longer. That is an important cultural reality.
On average we are more likely than ever to face decades of late-life
challenges. In the face of that changing circumstance more of us are
choosing a new October partner rather than face our last years alone.
As one who tells fictional accounts of those challenging times I have
explored the retirement dilemma confronting many of my peers.
Should they face their uncertain future alone or look for someone who
will walk those last miles with them?*

Here is a real win-win situation. Gil gets to follow a path he remembers having dreamed of. He loves it. He creates a world in which his
characters can face, act out, and successfully handle challenges he just
might deal with, too. And his readers find a whole new satisfying genre of
senior fiction that reflects their lives.

PULLING IT ALL TOGETHER

It was hard to schedule chats with **David W.** of Kissimmee, Florida. He is
a very busy sixty-three-year-old man. Our long conversations had to fit in
with a schedule that starts at 10 a.m. but usually ends at 2 a.m. By way of
introduction, he said,

*I live in a fifty-five-plus community, and ideas about retirement are all
over the place. Many people here are bored and will eventually die
young. Many volunteer or work at Disney World or Universal. The*

ones that are happy and healthy have a driving reason to get up in the morning and can be likened to the White Rabbit in Alice in Wonder- land. *Others make a career of bitching about anything and everything. Hard to understand.*

Why is that so hard for you to understand?

My biggest problem at this point in my life is time. I don't have enough of it and at the end of the day never get a fraction done of what I want to have accomplished. It might be technology, which is a major black hole [of activity] for me, or it might be racing to a finish line that doesn't exist that seems to stop me. I am fortunate that in the kind of work I do I make my own hours.

David's description of his days and evidence of his energy left me breathless. As his story unfolded, it became clear that he has managed through difficult years—years that include divorce, a protracted length of alcohol abuse, and survival of a traumatic accident in which two people were killed and David spent six months in bed followed by six more on crutches—to have the resilience to meet formidable obstacles, to over- come them, and to rise to new heights each time. When his activity was limited by his being on crutches, for example, he called his son's school and asked if he might volunteer there.

When a seventh grader asked, "How does AOL work?" David realized that the whole premise of a "computer class" was ineffectual and charac- teristically set about improving the situation. This led eventually to learn- ing how to create and deliver "Curriculum Using Technology" on a uni- versity level—now called e-learning—earning a doctorate, and teaching distance education, film, and instructional design.

Instead of the end of the line, each apparent stopping point has been a fork in the road for David. In a happy marriage now, with strong relation- ships with his grown son and daughter, he soberly pursues intellectually and emotionally satisfying interests. His energy is undiminished.

Have you ever retired from a particular career?

I'm in about my thirty-fifth now. With the possible exceptions of driv- ing a taxi in New York City, purchasing car parts for my father's business while living in China, and starting and running two mutual funds, the others all have a more obvious connection in communica-

tions. When I started out I wanted to act and did off–off-Broadway. My bachelor's degree—the "fallback" to please my parents—was in speech, theater, and English. After lengthy sidesteps in the business world, everything has been connected to those original and ongoing interests.

My motivation is usually being "pissed off" and thinking I can really do something better than what I find. I've always been a writer, which certainly applied to starting the first themed bulletin board system in northern New Jersey sixteen years before the Internet and running forums on CompuServe for over ten years as a hobby. I've also always loved reading to children. I read all fifty-six Oz books to my kids, plus everything else I could find. I love doing the different characters' voices.

And just what is this "thirty-fifth career" that brings so many of these threads together for you?

For the past two years I have prepared for, trained, and worked as a professional voice actor. Recording audible books is satisfying; voicing characters for video or film is exciting work. When I enrolled in a two-year program to prepare for this, I felt I had come full circle, using everything I have, know, and enjoy: performing, technical expertise, literary interests.

David scorns the whole idea of retirement, as do many others who view their whole lives as works in ongoing progress. His whole life seems to be in sync right now, with sufficient stimulation and challenge to provide the balance he needs. The challenge is in building the career he has figured out for himself and loves through the kind of promotion and marketing it takes. He knows he has the energy and drive necessary.

EXPRESSING THE MEANING

Perhaps the seeds were planted in his Presbyterian father's sermons in East Tennessee, where **John Victor Compher ("Vic")** was born in 1945, the second of five sons.

My parents believed that everything in your life has a purpose. This was deeply instilled in us.

Finding and expressing meaning in his life is surely a thread that has led to Vic's primary occupation as a filmmaker instead of being a retiree. Perhaps, also, there is a connection to his forebears, who came to this country from Germany in 1730, in the love of the German language he learned as an exchange student in Berlin and his eventual authorship of a book of poetry in German and English.[1] He has found ways to express the meaning he continues to find.

Vic was more used to being the interviewer than the interviewee, he told me as we had coffee in my kitchen in Philadelphia.

Was filmmaking ever a goal?

With a master's degree in German and having met my wife in graduate school, I thought we'd both be teaching German. But, no, that was my first adult disappointment. The rise of the student movement for academic freedom had changed the market: colleges stopped requiring foreign language. Social work was plan B [and an MSS at Bryn Mawr's Graduate School of Social Work]—a good one, as it turned out. That midlife career of over thirty-seven years was in child welfare, hospice, and clinical social work.

At each phase of this career, Vic proved to be committed and creative. He wrote about work with families[2] and came to recognize the effects of the kind of work he was doing on the lives of family caregivers, volunteers, and professionals as they dealt with the needs and traumas of others in their care.

I was deeply affected by working with children and families in which trauma and even death could and sometimes did occur. I was also deeply affected and challenged by "secondary trauma," which at the time I called "professional grief." I helped create an experimental "grief-assistance" program in Philadelphia's Department of Human Services that included peer counseling, support groups, and an annual day of remembrance. The notion of secondary trauma originated with dealing with veterans and recognition that the process of empathy requires self-care as well as the care for others.

The Bird Takes Wing

At fifty-five, I felt like a bird out of its cage. Away from the terrible pressure of the Child Welfare System, out of the office.

Vic was able to spread his wings, establishing a freelance career as a social-work trainer and social worker providing psychotherapy and bereavement counseling and creating a workshop that has reached thousands of professional caregivers throughout Pennsylvania and New Jersey. This gave him the freedom to pursue his interests in the arts, in interfaith relations, and in peace.

During this period I joined an artists' support group. I became a founding board member of Artwell—an arts program for youth in response to chronic community violence—Greater Philadelphia Interfaith Center, and cofounder of the Interfaith Walk for Peace and Reconciliation.[3] I went on a trip spending a week each in Israel and Palestine, conducted by a rabbi from Albuquerque and an African American imam who were inspired by Buddhist monks. We brought the rabbi and the imam to Philly and had our first Interfaith Peace Walk in 2004 and have done so every year since; four hundred to seven hundred people come. We meet every month in an effort to combat the divisions that have been promoted through propaganda since 9/11.

Filmmaking evolved from my writing. I was fascinated by the stories of people I met as a social worker and began writing their stories, but not as case studies and aside from academic papers and journal articles. In my early fifties, I thought I'd like to document the interesting people I met. I've always loved older people and found myself more and more interested in their stories. At age fifty-seven I produced and directed my first film, called Treasures of the Elders, *about older adults transitioning into a phase of their lives, discovering—like me!—their artistic capabilities. The second is called* Peace of the Elders, *about older adults involved in making the world a more peaceful place. The third,* I Cannot Be Silent, *is intergenerational—older people sharing stories with younger, inspired by a child psychiatrist, a Holocaust survivor at eleven, who only started telling his story in his sixties and started going to classes to tell his story to children.*

Full Flight

Today Vic has organized a professional team of videographers, editors, an animator, and a musician; created an advisory board; and formed Lifedream Films, LLC. His fourth film, *Portraits of Professional CARE-givers: Their Passion, Their Pain*, has been completed and launched in both full-length and short forms, gaining recognition and sparking conversation and action as it is seen. Despite the persistent myth that "real professionals are objective, unaffected emotionally, and heroic," Vic has seen that many caregivers suffer emotionally from contact with traumatized clients. He writes:

> *Professionals, lacking adequate self-care, support from colleagues, or organizations, may no longer be able to function at their best; some may become cynical, unhelpful toward clients, or angry about the demands of their jobs; others may retire or leave their professions prematurely. PTSD and significant suicide rates are well documented in some fields, especially among police, firefighters, and medics.*

Interest in others, caring for others, making the world a better place—it's all coming together for Vic in a way he couldn't foresee as a young man in East Tennessee. His story makes a good case for personal evolution.

HANGING LOOSE

At fifty-nine, **Sam R.** of Berkeley, California, found himself in what has become a fairly frequent position in Silicon Valley: jobless for the first time since college. With both bachelor's and master's degrees in electrical engineering, he had always held good, satisfying jobs. We were introduced by a mutual acquaintance and met in one of Berkeley's ubiquitous coffee shops. Sam looks very fit and no older than his age of sixty-one.

> *When my wife and I decided to stay out here after graduate school, it was great. She runs a nonprofit organization, and our two kids are out of college now and on their own. I started working as an engineer at HP. We could afford to buy a house—which we could never do out here today—and it's been a great place to raise children. By the time I was in my mid-thirties I had opportunities with start-ups that were*

really tempting. I bought into the ground floor on one and worked there for several years, but it never really took off. I started my own consulting firm with a couple of other engineers. We made a living, but nothing spectacular in Bay Area terms. Anyway, I was always very employable and could find pretty lucrative contract work in interesting places like Google, my last place. When my last project was finished there, I sent my résumé around the whole company, and, for the first time, I got not one response.

I really hated not working on a real project—having a real job. We can live on what we have, but I really need to keep busy, and I'm not ready to embrace what I used to think retirement meant. I'm handy. I can drive. And I like being paid. So I've been driving for Uber a lot, and now I'm signed on with TaskRabbit, which I'm actually enjoying. People who need things done go online, describe what they need—like building something, or computer work of any kind—and they find my name and an hourly fee. I've built up a small number of repeaters who know me now. Meanwhile, I still have my résumé out in case something "real" comes up. I've taken advice and removed my date of birth and a few early years of employment from the résumé. So far, no takers, but I'm still ready—sort of hanging loose.

Obviously, Sam doesn't consider what he is doing to be "real work." He is in that limbo where his profession seems to have left him behind and his kind of skills are sought accompanied by a very young face and a short résumé, particularly in his neighborhood. It will be interesting to check back with Sam in a few years and see what he's doing then. Still enjoying the variety of new-economy jobs? Finding and exploring new interests and activities? He lives in Berkeley, a cauldron of intellectual stimulation and political activism. Or maybe someone will respond to his application for work in his profession. A volunteer experience may open a whole new vista for Sam. He is likely to have another third of his life ahead.

AN UNEXPECTED (SUNNY) FORECAST

Woodrow B. of Philadelphia, Pennsylvania, has worked at the Hospital of the University of Pennsylvania for forty-two years. At the present time his job is to transport people from one part of the hospital to another. But he doesn't just move people around. He takes an interest in them and finds out about their lives, and in doing so he enriches their experience because they find in him a comforting, warm person who makes a scary hospital procedure a bit softer and more bearable. Woodrow and I had a lovely conversation as he was transporting me during a recent hospital stay. Focusing on our conversation rather than on the impending procedure was far better than depending on an opiate to calm me down.

> *I've worked here for forty-two years, and it's been a good place to work. But now I'm thinking of retiring. It gets to a point where money-wise it stops being a benefit to continue to work. I really like to cook. I've made barbecues for over one hundred people, and they are good! I'll be ready to retire in about two years, and cooking is what I'd like to do. I can take on cooking jobs when I want to and not do it if I have too much to do or just decide not to work right then. I've worked hard and steady all my life, and now I'm ready to just sit back and enjoy people and cooking and whatever else. The only thing that really bothered me recently is that I was mugged. These guys saw me in a uniform and knew I work and probably had some money on me. They broke my nose. See the marks? No, this isn't the first time. It happens in the neighborhood I live in. But I'm really looking forward to doing parties and cooking. That's happy work, and I like doing happy things with people. How about you? What do you do for fun?*

Woodrow and I had a pleasant exchange, and then we arrived.

> *Well, here we are, and good luck to you. I hope you do well, and I'm sure you'll get better. You're in a real good hospital.*

Woodrow was such a fresh flower in the sea of tubes and beeping computer screens that is a hospital. He was a real person with a real life and real feelings and real problems of his own who walked into my life for a few precious minutes, and I know he will have impact on others' lives as he did mine—when I really needed it. The forecast for Woodrow's coming years is sunny for him and the people fortunate enough to be in his orbit.

HOW ABOUT YOU?

Think about the forks in your road so far. When you do actually stop and think about them, there may appear to have been more than you realized. Where did each one lead? A dead end? A new idea? A whole new path or byway? Is there one you always kind of wished you had followed but didn't have time for? Make a list. Dream big. Maybe now *is* the time to follow a new path.

5

MEANDERING

Now, here, you see, it takes all the running you can do, to keep in the same place. If you want to get somewhere else, you must run at least twice as fast as that!

—Lewis Carroll, *Through the Looking-Glass*

Retirement? It's like I was given a card to Get Out of Jail Free. I think I've looked forward to retirement almost since I started working. I am one of those people who was never absolutely sure what I wanted to be when I grew up. So I took the path of least resistance and went into my father's tire business even though somehow being a grease monkey and kicking tires did not appeal. Yes, I could have built the business into something more, but I really didn't have the initiative or imagination, nor was I willing to invest the sweat equity it would have taken.

Bill N. and I were sitting in the well-tended garden behind his row house on a quiet street in Pittsburgh, Pennsylvania. Bill is obviously of modest financial means and has been retired for ten years. He closed his business when his own children went off to other places, other dreams. I asked him about his life now.

I'm actually a very contented man. I never really liked my work very much, but I had a family to feed, kids to educate, a wife to care for, and a mortgage to pay. Our home was—is—a happy home. My castle, really. I never shied away from hard work, and I never could let other people run my business. So I've worked long hours, often from 7 a.m. to 7 p.m. and later, and am now glad I don't have to be a slave to an unforgiving business any longer. I take care of my little backyard as though it's a big estate. I grow tomatoes and then pickle them. I started to play golf at a public course when I retired, and sometimes I just enjoy relaxing with a book or a movie. I belong to a service club in my community and go to meetings and do some volunteer work for them, although some people say they are not as powerful a group in the community as they once were. It probably sounds like a pretty boring life, and sometimes it is, but I'm happy. I guess I was always a kind of low-energy guy, and I'm glad nobody's pushing me anymore.

We didn't run into many people like Bill. People who are satisfied with quiet, unobtrusive lives that seem to make little mark on their world. But they're out there, and we hope they remain comfortable for the rest of their lives. They know who they are and that they owe no one an explanation.

WHAT'S THE NEW GAME?

What do we mean by "meandering"? We found lots of men who complained about the rat race they had been running during their working lives. Many spoke about the heavy workloads taken home, the interminable hours at the office, the punishing travel schedules, the relentless competition at the workplace, all those people eager to grab your advantage, your ideas. Men who feel, as the Red Queen told Alice, that you have to run as fast as you can just to keep up.

What is the real transition that a man faces as he approaches this chapter in his life?

- Does he find new worlds to control and conquer?
- Does he transition from control of his world of work to a life of leisure, relaxation—a letting go of the reins so that others can continue the job of whipping the world into shape?
- Does he sit back and coast, allowing himself to glide as the currents take him? New horizons, new adventures? Pursuing dreams deferred from an earlier time?

Some men seem compelled to continue along the familiar paths, finding different avenues but with the same destination. Competitive golf?

Home-management competition with their wives? A seat on the condo board? They seem unable to leave the world of control and competition, the game of politics, or the workplace behind them. Programmed from infancy, it's a game to be pursued. And happy are those who can do this gracefully and with emotional reward.

Other men slip easily and comfortably into relaxation and leisure— drifting dreamily into a stress-free time when sipping coffee, days on the couch reading or watching TV, and walking the dog before an afternoon nap seem like the perfect antidote to years of clock watching and deadlines to be meticulously met so that no one catches up to you from behind.

And then there is another way where men's fancies catch their eye and take them on paths they may pursue while those paths appeal to them and abandon when those interests no longer do. Exploration, not dilettantism!

LIFE ISN'T A MATTER OF EITHER-OR

Max B. of Philadelphia, Pennsylvania, told us that he is at times conflicted about how to handle the many options and opportunities that present themselves to him.

I've been under a lot of stress all my working life. Many, like me, just want to sit back and relax. We're tired of stress. Some don't feel healthy enough to handle so much stress much longer. Too much pressure. I want to spend my limited time with my grandkids or some other self-entertaining activity. It's time to pass on the baton.

My problem with the control area now is that I've always worked from eight to five. I went to my office with a mission. I worked at fulfilling the mission and then came home. Postretirement, there's no schedule. I set up the schedule. My biggest problem is my time allocation. So what I do is load two or three days a week and know what I'm doing those days. Today I'll be out of my house until 9 p.m. tonight! The rest of the week I take a little more care of myself. I go to the gym, I pick up my grandchildren from school, I do some landscaping for my son. I speak three languages fluently, so I was able to find work teaching ESL classes. Also, my former company called me back to do some part-time work for them.

Prepare! That's a buzzword for me. Maybe people should begin think-ing now, before they get to this life stage, what are their interests. I saw the handwriting on the wall when my employer in Brazil told me he was putting me under the guidance of the human-resources vice president. He was putting me on notice that retirement was around the corner. I'd seen this before, so my plan was to be financially solid. I was still paying off one mortgage. So I began to immediately start to plan with a firm date in mind, which I was fortunately able to stick to.

The fact that I'm not working is not a failure. For me, the biggest challenge is what I'm going to do for the next thirty years. For a third of your life you were building to become someone. The other third you did something, you worked, you built a family. Now my biggest prob-lem is, what are my next goals? What am I going to do?

I'm really of two minds about this business of how to spend my retire-ment years. I don't want to give up altogether doing what I consider worthy activities and just meander aimlessly through this next big stage in my life. But my second mind loves the relaxation. I think it has to do with attitude. Some seniors are passive; others take an active approach. Past life experiences play a huge role in this. Who they were when they were younger are who they are when they are older. I think the older seniors are looking to the younger seniors to lead. My pastor always says that great ideas come up, but often the people who bring up the great ideas don't want to lead, so you have to get involved yourself.

So what I've decided to do is spend two or three days in very struc-tured activity and the rest of the week in a freewheeling way. So far this dual approach works for me.

Max has some distinct advantages. He did not walk in cold to this stage of his life. He told us that he used his connections to his church, the human-resources office where he worked, and his abundance of initiative. He capitalized on where he was known and respected and where connec-tions already existed. Max "meanders" for part of the week and structures the remaining days, which satisfies his need for both.

Sam P., a retired Chester, Pennsylvania, high school American history teacher, learned over the course of his teaching career to adapt to the changes his students needed to make in finding and using resource mate-rials. He helped his local library organize its resource center for teachers and students as a volunteer. He continues to work there three days a week and finds that the interaction with students and teachers is rewarding and keeps him up-to-date on new technology and ideas.

I enjoy this so much; I'm putting together a résumé to send to museums in the area, offering to organize a resource/study center for them. I don't think they would pay since they have staff who could work with me, but I would not object to being paid! Anyway, I would do it without pay for the fun of it.

At seventy-five, **Alan G.** of Evanston, Illinois, and Montana has approached the third age and stage in his life on a path that veers far from the more stress-filled path he had traveled earlier. He and his wife have a cabin in the backwoods, and they spend the entire summer there.

It's a very remote place. There are people within a reasonable distance of our cabin. Five miles, ten miles, but our cabin is surrounded by the national forest in the western foothills of the Rockies near Glacier National Park. In the summer, I totally immerse myself in living in the middle of nature. I enjoy the trees, the sky, the wind, the stars. We hike, we canoe. We no longer white-water canoe. In deference to our age, we canoe on the lake. We go into town once a week to do our laundry and buy supplies. Our neighbors live five miles away in an adult senior community. There are twenty or thirty people that we relate to in various ways. And we have some friends in town. We've been doing this since the 1980s. It's a very laid-back life. When we go into town, we check our e-mail and do whatever business we have to do since we have no Internet at the cabin.

What was your life like before you retired? Do you feel you were defined by your work?

Well, at least for me part of retirement was that I never wanted my identity as an employee to define me whether or not I went from practicing law for twenty years to teaching law for fifteen years. Yes, I planned for retirement and who I would be when I retired even while I was practicing law. So I was comfortable moving from the practice of law to the teaching of law and then to stepping away from my career. I didn't feel I had to linger or lighten my teaching load or give random lectures. It's not that I had a plan worked out. I just knew that teaching was getting a little stale. If you can afford it, the time to stop working is an arbitrary determination, and I arbitrarily decided that age sixty was the right time for me. I never really anguished over what I would do at this stage of my life. I just slid into it. I stopped at the end of the semester and went to Montana, out in the woods where there's nothing to do.

I think that when I was practicing law, making a lot of money was important. And the value of being highly thought of. My craving for those values have fallen away. That isn't my particular interest. My particular interest is greater self-satisfaction, that I like doing what I've done in life, what I'm doing now, and that I've done it well.

Law practices and academia are not exactly arenas in which collaboration and cozy cooperation are known to be the norm. Yet you seem to have made the transition from pressured work life to a comfort zone that is enviable. You spend your summers in Montana, but how do you spend your winters in Evanston?

Our day usually starts with going to the Y for a swim. I also go over photos from my daughter's wedding and pictures from my trip to Australia. I don't know what I'll do with them anyway—just put them away, I guess. I like working on photography, particularly working on improving the pictures. My wife and I are very active in social-justice issues. We spend a fair amount of time gong to a vigil at a detention center for immigrants who are going to be deported. Our Jewish congregation has an interfaith vigil program one Friday a month. We get up at 5 a.m. to drive so we're there at 7:15 a.m. Evanston is a sanctuary city for immigrants, the last stop for so many unfortunate people before O'Hare Airport and deportation. We're working for a more humane immigration policy.

One day a week I spend an hour visiting a brain-damaged friend of mine, both socializing and working on his speech. And there are lots of items that need to be attended to in the details of our daily existence. Last night I spent the evening retrieving airline tickets for the trips we are taking in the next seven or eight months, like Montana in June. Detail work goes slowly, and I get satisfaction when it's done right.

Is Alan meandering? Like most men, he's doing a bit of meandering and scheduling his time, and he has managed to create for himself a third stage in life that is satisfying, rewarding, and meaningful.

I'M THE DESIGNATED SOCIAL BUTTERFLY, AND PEOPLE LOVE ME FOR IT

Mark S. of the Bronx in New York, New York, a handsome and vigorous ninety-two, was in show biz from the time he was a child. Of course, show business pushes and pulls you into a very different kind of life than the corporate, academic, or working-class existence does. There are lots of temptations out there that are hard to avoid. I asked Mark about his transition from life in the theater.

Probably after I sold my business, I floundered a bit before I found my footing again.

What business were you in?

First I was in show business, and then I opened up a gentlemen's boutique. I was a singer. I'm from Buffalo originally, and at that time I was studying opera and studying with the Buffalo Philharmonic Orchestra. I won a scholarship to the American Theatre Wing here in New York, and then I performed all over the country.

Then, when I realized I was getting older, life became hard on the road. I thought it was time to give up show biz and opened up a gentlemen's boutique shop in Riverdale. I always had worked part-time in men's shops as I was growing up to pay for my music lessons.

Well, I suddenly changed from my previous life. I've always been a very social person. We always had a lot of friends, many different circles of friends, and I wanted to continue centering my life around social activities.

When I lost my wife, that was a change of another part of my life. Unfortunately, one year ago I lost one of my daughters. The first six months I was a basket case and wandered around aimlessly. One morning I woke up, and I said to myself, "This has got to stop." I got cleaned up, got to the front door, put my hand on the handle, and said, "Okay, now where will you go?" I headed for the Jewish Y, about five blocks from my house, and started to go to the gym. I saw all these elderly people and said, "Dear God, I hope I'll never be in that position!" And, hello! Here I am! My friends keep me going, and that's how I spend my time. For a man my age, I'm very lucky. I go out with many couples. I'm the third one or the fifth one, and it doesn't bother me, and it doesn't seem to bother them.

Tell me what your day is like. What sorts of things do you do during the day?

The first thing is the Y, which saved my life. I get up in the morning, shower, dress properly, and go to the Y. I sit with this group. We call it Table 11. We're the liveliest ones in the whole place. Our discussions are wonderful, our jokes are terrific, and I travel and tell them stories about where I go and what I do. I did something with them. I asked them to each give me five dollars a week, I'll save the money, and when we have a certain amount we'll go to a very fine restaurant. They thought that was a great idea. We had the time of our lives at Sunday brunch. Then we upped it to ten dollars a week and did this more often. Everybody gets dressed up, and the conversation is different. Everybody is very bubbly. We get together for cocktails at each other's homes. I belong to a choral group that meets once a week and my men's club.

I've noticed a big change in these people. Their voices have a lilt, their eyes shine, they wouldn't miss our get-togethers for the world. I feel I am having an impact on them just by bringing them together as a group socially. Something is in their lives now that wasn't there before. I love being the catalyst of that. It makes me happy just to see them happy. I've had a wonderful life. I enjoyed everything I ever did, which most men can't say.

Mark is a retiree who has opted to meander at this time of his life. He is not continuing to use his singing or acting skills to see him through retirement. He has not ventured on new paths or pursued dreams unfulfilled. He actually has continued to do what he loves best—connect with people. He impacts their lives in positive ways, and that's where he gets his joy.

THIS WORKS FOR ME

Peter H. of San Francisco, California, formally retired on his sixtieth birthday from a major utility company after thirty years. He knew that downsizing was imminent and assured his superiors that as a single man he could probably handle early retirement more easily than colleagues who were raising families and facing college costs. He took the year-and-a-half severance package and has never regretted it. Never married, but often in a monogamous relationship, Peter sees some similarities to his life today when he looks back at his twenties. Both were unstructured times—like going back to the future.

I always kind of joke that I was getting ready for my retirement when I was in my twenties—kind of like Back to the Future—*because I really didn't work very much in my twenties, so I kind of got used to it. I'm not at all representative—having some activity, things to do, going to the gym, the wine business, personal relationships—these are what it's all about.*

Unlike kids today, I didn't come to California for a job. We'd had a big incentive to stay in school during the draft. When I graduated [an English major at Wisconsin] it was the first year of the lottery; luckily, I dodged the bullet with a high number. Only one of my friends went to Vietnam—with the Marines.

None of my friends thought about working. It was the sixties! We worked odd jobs, did what we wanted to do, always had enough money to pay the rent. (Sounds like I was retired then!) I had a beat-up old VW that I drove from the East Coast to the West Coast and back again. I could drive to New York for a penny a mile. I drove all the way down to southern Mexico and stayed for a couple of months; we never thought about money. If I needed a job, I had applied to a half-dozen temp agencies in San Francisco, and they'd send me out for a week here or a week there. I think there was this weird little window of time in the sixties when you could—and did—get by like this. My overriding ambition in my twenties was to drive a cab here in San Francisco, but I found out you had to be twenty-five, and I was still too young. When I was old enough I came straight back from Mexico, applied for the job, and drove a cab for a few years. I really enjoyed it.

Peter found the 1970s a maturing time, he said. He thought he should start thinking about what else he might do, took a civil-engineering program at the City College of San Francisco, and went to Nepal with the Peace Corps to do land surveying. He came back after six months when he became ill, lived with a girlfriend in Sonoma, worked in a small engineering firm, and not long after got the job that he stayed in for thirty years.

> *I think my mother was quite relieved that her son finally had a real job after about ten years out of college.*

Peter's workplace paid for his further education in city planning in the 1980s that UC Berkeley offered in downtown San Francisco, and eventually he also earned his MBA at night when his work and interest grew in the direction of economic development. His experience and growing expertise took him into work he enjoyed not only within the city but also throughout the state. When he retired, he had helped to develop and co-manage a vital economic-development program.

> *Retirement didn't affect me in any profound way. I remember feeling odd about being home during the day, during the week in downtown San Francisco. But I was seeing a woman who actually lived back in my hometown in Wisconsin. She was still working. We went back and forth for two years before breaking up. Just about then my old boss called and asked if I could help him out with the reorganization of projects that were badly understaffed. When I told him of my travel plans to France and England, he said, "Fine—we'll work around them." That led to enough work to keep me involved for a couple of years.*

> *About thirteen years ago I became interested in making wine with a group in a garage, and I took some classes at UC Davis. This wine is just for our own consumption. From that I got into a commercial winemaking venture. We call it SoMa Cellars—SoMa stands for South of Market, where I live in San Francisco—and produce it in Napa and in Bordeaux, France.*

> *I've also been in a relationship with a woman, Susan, for the past several years, who, like me, has never been married and has no children. We don't live together.*

> *Because I was on the board of directors of my condo building, which has about 233 units, I started going to meetings of citizens' advisory committees. I can get up in the morning, have coffee, read the paper, and then I have to think about the wine business, planning a trip somewhere, seeing Susan, or going to one of these meetings. I have to laugh at myself when I say, "I can't do that—I have to go to a meet-*

ing." I used to hate going to meetings at work. But this is all very interesting.

I go to classes at the gym with twenty- and thirty-year-olds every day. I've noticed over the last couple of years that I'm having a harder time keeping up. If I can keep that up as best I can and our little wine venture keeps going for the foreseeable future, and hopefully my relationship with Susan goes on, I'll be very happy.

STRIKING A BALANCE

Norman C.'s family was part of the Second Great Migration of African Americans from the South to the North. In their case it was from a tobacco farm in rural South Carolina to Philadelphia. Although his parents ran away to the North together, they reestablished and maintained ties to the Southern family. In those days, as Norman, now seventy-three, explained to me,

South Carolinians, among Afro-Americans, had owned more property than in any of the other Southern states. In that second migration people came to the same areas in the North, so the culture and community stayed with us—the family, the picnics, the activities. Every year, through childhood and adolescence, I spent the summer months in South Carolina. As I grew older, I was responsible for several younger children from our AME church as we took the train back to work on the farm. Some years our parents came for the last two weeks and we were all together. Everybody knew everybody. Relatives owned businesses as well as farms in the area.

As a teenager, if you did anything "bad," the call would go forth, from "home"—South Carolina—to New York, to Connecticut, to Philadelphia: "We know what you did!" There was constant surveillance. Behavior was always monitored. Even two years later, you'd hear, "I know what you did."

Getting together was important. At one time I could count eight different reunions to attend in the South. But tradition has changed. My eldest child is forty-six and hasn't been down there since he was a child. We called ourselves city folk and country folk.

I can still recall, when I was about four years old, the shock of seeing an aunt come to our house wearing pants.

I first met Norman when I visited a writing group, The Best Day of My Life So Far, at the Philadelphia Senior Center. At seventy-three, Norman, who lives alone since his divorce years ago after twenty-two years of marriage, plans the elements of what appears to be a multifocused life to a satisfying and exemplary degree. And planning is definitely part of his way of life. His memory is prodigious, as is his knowledge of history, people, and, most important, himself. Talking with Norman is special; he tells stories as though he is writing them, with incredible grace and attention to his listener.

Norman has vivid memories of school.

> *I wasn't a good student in everything, but I always loved to read. I remember Miss Chase, my kindergarten teacher. I loved her. She said, "Norman knows his nursery rhymes better than anyone in the class." But I was shy and didn't do well after that. I do remember when my poem was on the bulletin board in third grade. I kept looking at it.*

> *When I was flunking typing in high school my aunt gave me her old heavy typewriter. I had to keep stopping as I took it home, and I practiced all weekend after church. By semester's end I was in the champion group. This told me that if I kept plugging, I could learn what I needed.*

So did you finally get into your own? A comfortable groove?

> *When I went to Bluefield State College in West Virginia I was disappointed, disillusioned, homesick, and thought I was failing. Then my first transcript came, and I did pretty well! I transferred to Cheyney University, pledged a fraternity, got into the civil-rights movement, did well in social studies, which I loved, and "came into my own," graduating early.*

> *Traditional black colleges in those days gave you lots of help. If they saw you were struggling but trying, they provided hours of tutoring. They might let you help in the garden, then sit down with you, for instance. We had instructors in black colleges who couldn't teach at places like Penn but had come out of there and really were the cream of the crop as teachers.*

In those days, how did your work fit into the draft? This was a major issue for young men in those days.

[Laughing] I was qualified for social studies and English when I came out of school, so of course I was placed in junior high math. I learned something, at twenty-two, about how privileges worked then. My principal offered me a place in a master's program in math. I also was accepted by the Peace Corps. It was likely I would be drafted if I didn't take one of those paths, and I really was a conscientious objector at first. However, I realized that I really couldn't do that, because I would be willing to fight for my family. So I was drafted, trained for the military police, and spent two years in Panama.

When I came out, I worked two jobs, subbing all day and working at a reformatory after school. (As a long-term sub, I won the argument with the school district over salary owed, after researching the law and finding the district had not sent proper notification.) I was married at twenty-six and purchased a house. When I stopped at the new house to let in a utility person, a policeman stopped and, even though he saw the deed I had with me, he took me to jail for two hours, although I had to be at work.

Preretirement work was not only in the public schools but also, simultaneously, as a probation officer and a parole agent. I like to strike a balance between what I think of as the intellectual and the physical side in my life. So for seventeen years I went "from white collar to blue collar" every summer in Ocean City, Maryland, doing labor—lots of heavy lifting—for restaurants in the seafood season.

How about today? Has your life changed from then to now?

I've been coming to this senior center for six years. At first I thought, "I'm too cool for this." But I had no computer then, and I came to use one here. I was doing research about basketball history—just because I was interested. An older white man kept encouraging me to come to Benita Cooper's writing class.[1] Eventually I wrote about this and apologized for my reluctance. I took a short course to refresh my grammar. Now I go to four different centers—for a poetry group, another Best Day class, and line dancing. It's good exercise and moves me into a social life. I meet people this way.

I write and take courses at Drexel University now.

People should look into senior centers. No matter what your interest is, you'll find it. I remember seeing my grandmother, forty years ago, taking the little yellow bus to the center every week, working on quilts and doll babies. You can't just sit around. I get up in the morning, and it's like going to school for me. I knew a man who never had a drinking problem until he retired. You have to keep your mind active.

Blow away those myths about not being old. You are! But that's okay!

SOME NICHES ARE HARDER TO FIND

Roland L. of Philadelphia, Pennsylvania, retired as a social worker when he was still young at sixty-two. He was actually forced to leave his job because of a physical condition having to do with a sleep disorder. He is the only child of deceased parents to whom he is grateful for their upbringing and support, and he feels blessed to have been able to help them as they aged. Roland lives alone and was never married.

When I retired twenty years ago, I lost my mother and my last parent. I was going through emotional setbacks and trying to deal with that. I had some serious issues with a sleep disorder, falling asleep at work, and I was finally let go. I had been at the job for over twenty years. I was a social worker, both in geriatric and health care. I said to myself, "I can't go back to work. I have to get treatment." My job was a hard environment in which to thrive. Where I worked, they didn't give you any type of reward, bonus, or recognition for your efforts. You had to achieve satisfaction from your own perceived accomplishments and your value to your client. My reward was recognizing my own inner strength and making contributions to service for others. I do find this better than a plaque, knowing that I did my best for others.

But now that I was out, I wondered where I was going to go. Doing volunteer work is scary, because you don't know if or how it will work or whether it will continue. I found the Senior Center in the Park—or, rather, it found me.[2] We call it the Gem in the Park, and it has worked out well. I get much gratification in the work from my new leadership role at the senior center. But there have been many unsettling times, many days of concern about what my future will hold. There still are.

You asked me about control and competition in a man's world. Being a social worker was a position dominated by women, and I can't imagine what a very aggressive, outspoken man would do in a workplace filled with women. He would not last long. However, I was not raised as that type of a person. I was not taught to always show my manhood.

I was taught to compromise, show compassion, understanding. Aggression, rivalry, reticence about my feelings were not valued in my profession. I would not really have been accepted if I had shown those kinds of traits when I was working. The skills I have been using since I retired have been the gentler ones. And I like it that way. I don't know that I think of my life as meandering. It's certainly a more relaxed life than many experience. I guess I'm still looking.

A CRITICAL VIEW

Tom L. and his wife are still living part of the time in New York, New York, until she completes work toward her own retirement as a school psychologist. Meanwhile, he is establishing their next home and his footing in Philadelphia. Tom, at sixty-one, was the youngest member of the group we met at the Philadelphia Corporation for Aging. He had already been retired for two years. His provocative observations about aging and the experience he is having as a volunteer at Journey's Way in Philadelphia made me eager to talk to him further. We had coffee together at my home. As we talked, Tom made notes frequently and referred to his own. He has a delightful sense of humor and connection, but it's clear he is a serious man, whatever the topic.

All of Tom's experiences so far have seemed to point the way to his current apparent meander. His parents, both Chinese, met as college students in the United States. His father, a young physician, died before Tom could know him. Tom and his two brothers were raised by his mother and her white American husband in upper-middle-class towns in New England and the South, where he was always the only Chinese boy in his class. Even in his small, Quaker, liberal-arts college, he was one of only three.

Even in college, the others were a Malaysian Chinese and a Peruvian Chinese. We all had very different identities. I went into the Peace Corps, to the Philippines. I had no clue. I didn't know they really disliked the Chinese. Also, they had this sort of worship of white Americans—considered whiteness aristocratic. I didn't know this, and I basked in the sun. Within three months my skin was much darker and I looked Filipino and had no sense of being special. The experience colored my sense of being American. But apparently I caught some attention, and when I returned to the States I was asked to work as a recruiter for the Peace Corps in Boston. They thought I had some talent for "corralling people." Being Chinese had something to do with that in the late seventies when there was an interest in recruiting Asians. (Now it's almost reversed.) For so many years I was very tuned in to Asian-born or American-born Asians, people who grew up isolated and don't speak the language.

A career in a successful architecture firm in New York was unsatisfying and unfulfilling, lacking in opportunity for actual design work, and filled with tasks Tom found meaningless. With his wife's encouragement, he returned to the academic world and success in admissions and recruitment programs. Tom's skill set, including his talent for "corralling people," was immediately appreciated.

I became the director of a program in Brooklyn which offered three years at the college and direct entry to medical school. I found quota requirements, rejections of highly qualified students, and political pressures hard to bear and resigned after two years. I moved over to another university's business and then MBA program for six years, making eleven trips to China, India, Israel, and Turkey for them. Again, the politics became intense. I still haven't resolved issues of inclusion for myself.

Able to retire, we decided to relocate in Philadelphia, and I looked around for things to do, not just to stay busy. I was influenced by a book I picked up in the library.[3] And I found a website for Journey's Way, which offered services and programs for people over fifty-five. I reached out to them, applied, and went into a training program.

What are you learning?

I really don't like being called a "group leader." I prefer "facilitator" working with the group of seniors who meet regularly at Journey's Way. We're learning, too. For some, it's so important to be "leaders." We're not there to make anyone feel different about their own lives; no, we're there to develop our own sensitivity to their experiences. Men are so anxious to hold on to some title, to feel "I've got a place in this world." If anything, I'm learning more from this group because they're older and I've actually gotten some clues about living.

I find it repugnant that so much of what we celebrate and hold up as models about being old is running marathons or other great physical achievements. One of the realities of aging is that our bodies do wear. There is a time to recycle—to get the most out of our heads. When I go on one of my regular walks along the Wissahickon I see "old-timers" struggling to run, and I think, this has got to be completely unhealthy for them, but they must feel that they have to do it to "stay young."

Teaching an ESL—English as a Second Language—class, at another center, has me thinking like an English teacher, talking about past, present, and future. In the senior group, we talk about the present, and it's all about illnesses, coping, dealing with loneliness. We're not psychologists. I realize we're almost trying to entertain. For the past, I put together slides of old movies, events, et cetera, from the thirties and forties. Let's reminisce. Goes wonderfully. But what about the future? Maybe it's that Asian side of me that thinks there's much more than this.

So many older people are very lonely. We keep hearing platitudes about how wonderful it is to have this time to spend with children and grandchildren, but at least 60 percent of people don't have that in their lives. For those who don't have that to hang on to, what gives meaning to their lives? Most of the group, when I asked, I learned would be coming to the senior center for Thanksgiving dinner.

There is no cycle in this culture. It just sort of ends. Maybe it's because I'm younger that I see this. Where is the future? This to me is so critical. It's like a tree: You have the seed, the sapling, the tree, the blossoms, the fruit. The apple falls, and you have the seed again. It's all contained in the seed. The seed has everything that allows us to come forth again. What gives meaning to this path that we're on? For many men, it's saying they have children; it shows their virility. But that's not true for so many. Men really do have to hold on to these anchors: what my career was, who my children are.

Is this what you expected?

Given my interest in art and design, I thought I would do more reading and start using my hands again. I developed an eye condition, being monitored, in the last year and a half that interferes with acuity in one eye. Now I appreciate this free time.

"Meander" takes its meaning from the fabled river in Turkey that twists and turns over many miles before it reaches the Aegean Sea. Tom seems to be plunging into a sea of learning, meaning, and promise for himself and others.

A TIME FOR CONTEMPLATION

A very youthful seventy-two, **John Santa** of Marion, Montana, is beginning to realize the full implications of retirement for him. For one thing, he is aware of physical changes when he skis with eight- and ten-year-old grandchildren, whom he helped learn how to ski, and can no longer keep up with them. When I talked to John, he was still transitioning from the multileadership positions he has held at Montana Academy, a therapeutic boarding school for teenagers he founded with a psychiatrist partner twenty years ago. Succession has been in the planning for five years to ensure the continuation of the school in a way that maintains its mission and integrity. John's wife, Carol, involved professionally from the academy's beginning, has had a head start on developing outside interests and activities. John told me:

> For high achievers, retirement leaves a big hole. I went straight through college and graduate school and was a tenured college professor at twenty-six and had published twenty articles. Then Carol and I moved back to Montana, and I went into the restaurant business with my brother. Within several years I was back in school for another PhD, in clinical psychology—really a "retraining program without another dissertation"—and did a postdoc internship in neuropsychology at San Diego. Then I went into private practice before founding the school.

> The big job is that I've run my life around achieving and accomplishing—and the biggest challenge for me is to come to grips with being, not necessarily accomplishing, and being okay about that. Each time I shifted careers I established another goal of what I'd do. This time is different. It's the first time I don't see my job as having another goal of something to accomplish in retirement. How do I quit trying to achieve things and just be?

> Part of aging is you really do have to face the finality and vulnerabilities, things you don't face when you're young and active and all

future-oriented. What we find with these kids that we work with is they come to us with all these symptoms. They're depressed or suicidal, or they drink too much or use drugs—all sorts of behavioral and emotional symptoms. But the underlying problem is that they're really immature. They're little kids and don't have realistic ways of linking their present to their future. In our society you have to learn how to be an adult, to be your own person, to separate, to have goals that are realistic, that you could achieve. And that's what it means to grow up: to have realistic goals and aspirations.

At the other end, you have to say, "Well, I don't think I should be so future-oriented." To be part of this world when you're younger, you have to be operating with a future orientation. But as you get older, you have to not do that, because if you're constantly worried about the future, at a certain point the future is that you're going to die.

John, you're likely to have a long time ahead! Have you prepared for that? Are you giving much time to this next stage in your life?

Carol and I travel a lot. We basically want to stay here in Montana, not move to Arizona or a retirement community. We've taken major trips—hiking in Patagonia and Turkey, for example. I imagine we'll be doing more of that as we step out of focusing so much on the school. But we don't want to say, "That's what we do—we travel."

I'm somewhat of an activist. Carol and I just wrote an article/opinion letter to our local newspaper about the appalling stance of our community government regarding the acceptance of any immigrants. We wrote a quasi-religious letter quoting biblical verses and saying, "What would Jesus say?" We're very interested in politics, find it stimulating and entertaining. I get involved locally with that. I've never been good at hobbies. I'm thinking of writing a book about the experience with the school.

I really think I'm just at the beginning of what I'm going to do as I age. I just don't know. Is it going to be doing something or learning how to be? I hope that if you take away the achieving part, there are still many interesting things to learn about. I hope it evolves in that direction. I'm not religious, but I feel I've acquired some system of belief that is pretty consistent with Judeo-Christian ethics. I value people, the environment, the world we live in. I feel it's important to contribute to it.

THE PATH IS CLEARING

We first met **John Creveling** and his wife, Christina Robertson, more than five years ago at a monthly lunch discussion-group meeting of a dozen or so more-or-less regular attendees who are all interested in aspects of "Positive Aging." It was not until years later that we learned that John had at that time recently been diagnosed with Parkinson's disease (PD). He was still fully engaged in the successful career-management consultancy he and his wife formed and have run together during their twenty-five-year marriage. John nears seventy very aware of changes PD has brought through physical and emotional or psychological challenges. Here's a shortcut to John's attitude toward life in general:

I hate the word can't! *It stops everything. I love the word* wow!

The youngest of four, John was a teenage husband, father, and US Army volunteer. He spent five years in the army.

> *I had volunteered for the infantry and was sent to NCO school and advanced NCO school, but I also had volunteered for Germany. So I was a Vietnam vet but never went to Vietnam. I still have survivor's guilt.*

The intervening years brought college, divorce, the business world, world travel, and an ever-widening perspective.

> *I define myself, in our culture, as a Christian, but not following any one dogma or church. I think of myself as a spiritual Christian. Buddha can be "God," for example. As a kid, I was homophobic, but I've evolved. Our travels have made me realize how much we have in common with people from other countries, other cultures. Globalization is changing the perspective of young people with the advent of the Internet. It's hard to understand why it doesn't make people more progressive in their thinking.*

> *One of the benefits of aging is you feel free to advocate for what you believe—care less about what others think when you feel strongly about what's right. I spent five years in the military and went to my first protest—against the war in Iraq. It felt important to stand there. I don't always feel good about our government's decisions. It felt good to stand there—silently. In the past I wouldn't have done that.*

Now approaching seventy, the Parkinson's diagnosis brought unforeseen changes, yet not all for the worse. In an interview in *Neurology Now*, John said,

> *This is definitely going to affect my riding a motorcycle into my senior years! I always dreamed I was going to be an octogenarian riding my motorcycle across America.* [4]

There may be no motorcycle, but this will no doubt be a ride—just a different kind. John told me,

> *Parkinson's disease doesn't define me. I was frightened by the diagnosis, realized how little was known, and how little progress there was toward a cure. But I focused on advocacy and support for research. Last year I had deep brain stimulation. I called it my rebirthing day. There are days when the medication doesn't kick in as well, when I have to think about it more. Now I say "carpe diem."*

The day John seizes now is usually full of activity—drawing, painting, photography, and writing, as well as physical movement, much of it expressive of his worldview, his appreciation of beauty and nature, and his inward journey. His "survivor's guilt" finds expression in a poem that he wrote following his visit to the Vietnam Veterans Memorial in Washington, DC.

The Wall

> *I've never been able*
> *to just look at "The Wall,"*
> *or simply walk by.*
> *I, who am alive,*
> *acknowledge those I once knew,*
> *among the 58,282 names etched in stone.*
> *Faces and names I promised myself*
> *I would never forget,*
> *but I have.*
>
> *They were dreamers, too,*
> *who dreamt of love, marriage,*
> *children, and family.*
> *They had aspirations, ideals, ambitions.*
> *Never to be attained.*

When we were kids my cousin Danny and I
liked to imagine we were musketeers.
Never far from home
we would run in the fields,
up and down the hills into the valleys,
off to rescue damsels in distress.
His name is there, etched for eternity.
His son never to know his father.
A father never to know his son.

I pause at this sacred place,
The Wall.
I bow my head,
close my eyes,
and always,
always, honor,
and keep in my heart,
those once young,
who lived as we do now.

Once ordinary,
now heroes all.
I wish they weren't. [5]

EYES WIDE OPEN

The life until now of **Oliver St. Clair Franklin**, OBE, has traced a meandering path through his seventy-one years of careers, social movements, and trenchant observations of an ever-changing world. The Order of the British Empire is an honor just below knighthood, which an American cannot be given. The honor was bestowed on Oliver in 1999 at the British Embassy in Washington. He is still Her Majesty's Honorary Consul in Philadelphia. We first met more than thirty years ago, when Oliver was the deputy city representative for arts and culture for the mayor and we were starting the Philadelphia Young Playwrights Festival. Over twenty years ago, when he was senior vice president of an investment bank in Boston, he participated in the World Symposium on Family Literacy at UNESCO in Paris, which I organized. Today he is the active executive of a research and design consultancy firm headquartered in Philadelphia.

Born in the segregated Freedmen's Hospital in Washington, DC, now part of Howard University Hospital, Oliver led a childhood off, not in, the streets of Baltimore, Maryland, where his father was a well-regarded pastor.

My father worked twenty-four/seven. None of us three boys became preachers. I considered it seriously until I realized how hard my father worked. Many family vacations were interrupted because Mrs. So-and-So died "and, Reverend, you know you have to preach the funeral!" And I really didn't believe in all of it. My father wasn't a "strict constructionist"—he believed in the importance of the social structure and position of the church in the community, in civil rights. It was a large church. We had a credit union. Scholarships for kids. That's what he enjoyed, not thinking about the number of angels on the head of a pin. My parents led in the effort to desegregate the public schools in Baltimore. Our church was in the middle of the black community, with middle-class and poor membership. Black doctors and lawyers lived there then among mostly two-parent families.

And was yours a desegregated education?

Hardly. I went away to Voorhees, in Denmark, South Carolina, an all-black school, now an accredited college, and which has a long affiliation with the Episcopal Church. Then I attended Lincoln University, my favorite school of all. I never attended school with white students until I went to Oxford after graduating from Lincoln with a degree in economics. I found I was well prepared and graduated from Oxford [on a Woodrow Wilson fellowship] with a degree in politics, philosophy, and economics. It was pretty amazing; I was there with a few Americans who actually talked about becoming president one day [Bill Clinton and Bill Bradley among them]. And Christopher Hitchens was a classmate and friend.

So how does your world look from here?

Pat [Oliver's psychologist wife] and I met in 1968, and I moved here to Philadelphia to be with her. The assumption was that the marriage wouldn't last because we were an interracial couple. Black women actually accosted me on the street. But, of course, the interracial side was only surface. We've been together ever since. The changes have happened so fast it even took me by surprise—seeing interracial cou-

ples on TV. Same-sex-marriage acceptance pales in comparison, but I'm glad to see it.

Getting older gives me a perspective, makes me reflect. Thinking about events in my lifetime is making me go back to biographies of people of the time. With all the technology at our fingertips, I feel seventy is the new sixty-two or sixty-three. When I used to think of someone being seventy, I literally thought of them as old. I'm at the gym in the mornings. I understand I can't compete with the younger guys. "Living long is winning the race!" Pat tells me. She says, "Get over it," if I complain. I'm still surprised when a really young person comes to work at our office and addresses me by my first name, but it's okay.

Now I understand what is meant by health. When you start to see people going [dying] around you, you think differently. Recently I did some work in South Africa. Someone approached me to get involved in a new project there, saying it's a ten-year project, at which time it pays off. I was mature enough to say I think this is something for people your age and turned it down.

The thing people of my generation worry about is Alzheimer's.

The very unretired Oliver Franklin's advice on retirement is:

If you're contemplating retirement, think of it as turning the page over for a new chapter. And think of whatever your passion is. You cannot not be engaged. You stand a better chance of living longer and happier if you're a social animal. Figure out what you can do to make a difference for the better. And take the physical side seriously. I have a wife who constantly reminds me that I'm getting old. You need that mirror [Pat] to tell you sometimes.

ABOUT MEANDERING

History tells us that it was Socrates who said, "The unexamined life is not worth living." If you're meandering, take a good look at your life, past and present. You may find the key to the new focus to calm your restless search in this new phase of life. Otherwise, do something connected to the wider world around you, and you are sure to find it there. The meander itself is worth the trip.

Sometimes what feels like a transition turns into something more permanent, an actual prolonged stage you find no reason to end. For some, it's a time of trying new activities that seem to morph into commitments. For others, it becomes a time of pleasant dalliances and unexpected discoveries. For anyone, it can be a time of getting to know yourself better than you thought you could. If searching produces anxiety, it may be a time to draw a deep breath and add meditating to your quiver of skills.

6

MY LIFE AT HOME FEELS DIFFERENT

The difference between a house and a home is like the difference between a man and a woman: it might be embarrassing to explain, but it would be very unusual to get them confused.
—Lemony Snicket, *Horseradish*

A WORLD IN FLUX

Oh, the confusion! Wasn't life simpler in most of the twentieth century, when roles were more clearly defined by gender? When change, if it happened, happened slowly, gradually—or so it looks in retrospect. Your fathers or grandfathers marched off to war or to limited conflicts around the world, or to work, while most of your grandmothers or mothers were still staying home, "manning" the factories for them or quietly doing good works and raising the children, about half of whom were boys whose fathers were absent for years, or at least all day long.

When a husband refers to his wife as "the little woman" today, he does so in jest—or at least pretends to be joking. Among the many things your gender has been expected to man up to, the liberated woman is one of the most affecting. We have only to look at today's young boys, teens, and Millennials to see their dramatically more gender-neutral world of school and the workplace. Now everyone is raised to be *allowed* to work in every field—they are even *expected* to work at something in addition to managing home and family responsibilities. So much is blurred. The sharp edges of differentiation—of roles, of society's expectations, even of aspects of what we thought of as gender—have softened.

Even time feels different. Work hours vary; families juggle schedules and responsibilities, sharing chores once divided into masculine and feminine categories. The newly retired man, or the man approaching retirement years, has probably noticed and experienced fallout from the changes in his partner's life and expectations. Can the couple still be in sync? Were they ever?

In the traditional family model of man and wife, or even in the more updated unmarried couple, the distaff side, or an implicitly designated partner, assumes the role of social secretary. Are you among the unusual men who have sent the holiday cards? Remembered birthdays? Sent gifts to the kids? Visited the sick or infirm on your own? Made the foursome dates for dinner or a movie? If you are alone for the first time since you were in your third or fourth decade, you may be conscious of a change in the fabric of your social life. Maintaining important relationships may be in your own sphere of responsibility for the first time. Are you up for the responsibility?

How are boys being raised to be men today? Is it different from when you were a boy? Is most of the change you see superficial, or does some of it actually get to what we have always thought of as innate? The *essence* of male and female—how much is what is expected because of gender, and how much is learned behavior? And how is the Longevity Revolution affecting how men and women are living with—and without—each other? What about "'til death do us part"? Still working for you in a time when the end of life gets much further away than when those vows were written?

After all, "Monogamy was created when men only lived to be thirty-nine years old."

We first heard that from the cynical veteran of a fifty-year marriage in a conversation almost thirty years ago. We might add that he is still married (more than fifty years) to the same woman, but what may have been mock ruefulness turns out to have been prescient to a degree, considering the growing impermanence of marriage. If you are the parent or grandparent of people in their twenties and thirties, you are doubtless aware of changing aspects of marriage. Median ages for first marriages have gone up seven years for women and six years for men since 1960 and are rising fast. Not only are people marrying later, but many more are not marrying at all. The traditional view of marriage you probably grew up with is also changing fast. These younger attitudes and shifting views of the institution of marriage are reflected in the culture surrounding us, as well as in hard statistics where we find longevity and marriage sometimes not meshing the way they used to.

DIFFERENT SCHEDULES, DIFFERENT LIVES?

Women have joked, "I married him for better or worse but not for lunch." The transition when one retires and the other doesn't isn't always smooth. For some couples, constant togetherness in work time, coupled with child-rearing, before retirement leads to a discomfiting realization that finally being together with so much unstructured time isn't all that great. Sometimes what appeared to be unbreakable bonds become brittle when the structures keeping them together are removed.

Alfred Stillman and Paula made their partnership work even when it meant moving around the country for her career and sometimes-difficult readjustments for his. The strains could be considerable, but the determination was strong on both their parts.

When two working people retire, they may plan to move together, as we learned **Tom L.** and his wife are doing in chapter 5. Tom retired first, with his wife's encouragement, but she has a few more years before her retirement makes sense financially. They decided to buy a house in Philadelphia and maintain both residences—in Philadelphia and New York—until then, spending weekends together as Tom pursues new pathways in Philadelphia and his wife awaits her own transition.

When **Alan G.'s** wife retired eight years before he did, she encouraged him to retire as well. You encountered Alan, now a wood turner, in chapter 4.

At the time we talked about how much fun we could have together and the things we could do, but I just felt my career was going well, and I just wasn't ready. When I did retire, my wife had her life taken care of. I think she was scared to death that when I retired all of a sudden she would need to entertain me or something like that. My wife is very active, has things to do all the time. She's the kind of person who can get on a bus and two stops later has three friends. When I first retired, I did go to events or activities with her and her friends a couple of times. It just didn't work. Not that I don't like the people. It's just a different type of conversation, a different focus on things. That didn't make sense. We took a film class together during the day, and part of it might have been that the teacher didn't do a good job, because pretty much they just showed us the movies. I didn't feel like sitting in a dark room at eleven o'clock in the morning.

Just by luck, I found out about a softball group before I retired—men and women, though mostly men, of a wide variety of ages, who meet to have informal softball games on Saturdays. I love sports, and I love to play softball, but most of the opportunities are in these leagues where everything is very serious and people really want to win and all that. With this, whoever shows up, they do their best to structure teams that seem to be even, and then you play. Actually, when one team starts to get too far ahead, they'll trade people to try to make it even. It's a fun group, and some of us always meet for lunch afterwards.

These people have become friends to the extent that through them I also started to play doubles tennis with a group of them. Some of the also-retired folks and others with more flexible schedules decided to start meeting on Wednesdays for softball batting practice. Then we'll go out to lunch. It's been terrific. One or two of them are semiprofessional musicians who do gigs on the side. We all try to attend them when we can. That has been a great source of people. It's absolutely true that I can have the types of relationships I couldn't have when I was working. It takes time and interest.

Full lives—for both Alan and his wife. So many different interests, so much of interest to share still. No one forcing himself or herself into a pattern that doesn't fit.

Mark Peterson and his wife, Carol (you'll be meeting Mark again after his "retirement at sixty," in chapter 8), realized he became a feminist early in their marriage when their first son was born. When Carol looked for part-time work, she was often told, "We don't take part-time people." He noticed, too, other men who apparently felt they were somehow above some of the demands of parenting, saying, "I'll change the wet ones, but I won't change the dirty ones." After years of teaching at universities and training mental-health counselors in New England, Mark and Carol shared their private psychology practice—Mark working with men, and Carol with women—and occasionally seeing patients, including couples, together before the two first retired at sixty to travel.

Even after divorce, **Bob R.** and his ex-wife Wanda have maintained practical and friendly cooperation:

> *When Wanda has appointments with doctors in San Francisco, she comes down here and stays in the house, and I can go up to her place. While I'm up there I'll work on her house if it needs fixing.*

Wanda, remember, is still his go-to person for confidences and advice.

BETTER OFF MARRIED?

Differences have been noted statistically of the difference marriage makes for men versus for women. Magazine advice to "marry, and you will live longer" is not necessarily true. (As one happy bachelor put it, "It will only seem longer.") Friedman and Martin, in *The Longevity Project: Surprising Discoveries for Health and Long Life from the Landmark Eight-Decade Study*, noted that marriage was beneficial in terms of health for men "who were well-suited for marriage and had a good marriage." For the rest, there were all sorts of complications. On the other hand, women who got divorced or stayed single often thrived. Even women who were widowed often did exceptionally well. Men who had gotten and stayed divorced were at high risk for premature mortality.[1] Makes you think, doesn't it? (Time for the joke about the partner who looks great after a divorce and explains, "I got rid of 180 pounds.")

CREATING HOME

When Robert Frost famously wrote, "Home is the place where, when you have to go there, they have to take you in," it's unlikely he had in mind today's homes, which are often way stations for people who are otherwise engaged—unless, as for many boomers and their elders, it's also the main workplace. Suburban living is less inviting than it used to be and dwindling for both over-sixties and Millennials. When the children have grown, or not yet arrived, the usual reasons for suburban life—backyards and school systems—no longer apply, and cities have so much more to offer in cultural, social, and health resources. Home is also, increasingly, the place for the single person, whose presence in the population continues to grow. The good news is that choosing to not marry no longer carries the social stigma it did in your parents' time. How and whether home consists of a couple or a family, same or mixed genders or generations, or one person with or without pets is part of the world in flux.

When people do marry or commit to one another, whether they live together or separately, the relationship is increasingly likely to be one of partnership, not ownership. They may remain financially independent of each other or consciously split responsibility for the expenses of living. It is just as likely, or more, for intimacy rather than proximity, for the emotional rather than the actual physical space to be occupied, to define a sense of "home." It may be more a state of consciousness based on the presence or availability of the person you're closest to.

TRENDS

We confess: sometimes we find statistics really boring. Not these, however! Actually, we are condensing what we've learned from the US Census Bureau's Current Population Survey for you so that your consciousness of this extraordinarily fast-moving society will be as awakened as our own. Some of these figures may come as a shock!

- There are now more Americans age sixty-five and older than at any other time in our history.
- The sixty-five-and-older population jumped 15.1 percent between 2000 and 2010, compared with a 9.7 percent increase for the total US population.
- People age sixty-five and older now make up 13 percent of the total population, compared with 12.4 in 2000 and 4.1 in 1900.
- Women significantly outnumber men at older ages, but the gap is narrowing. In 2010 there were 90.5 men for every one hundred women among people sixty-five and older, up from 88.1 men per one hundred women the same age in 2000.
- Between 1980 and 2010 the centenarian population increased by 65.8 percent. (We remember when turning one hundred earned you a birthday card from the White House—or at least from Willard Scott.)

- The proportion of Americans who live alone has grown steadily since the 1920s, increasing from roughly 5 percent then to 27 percent in 2013.
- The growth in population living alone in the fifty-five to sixty-four age group has nearly doubled since 1999. The increase is from 13 percent to 21 percent, surpassing even those seventy-five and older, who had been the largest component of those living alone in 1999.
- Fifty-one percent of people seventy-five and older live alone.
- About one-third of adults ages forty-six through sixty-four were divorced, separated, or had never been married in 2010, compared with 13 percent in 1970.
- In 2010 about 12 percent of unmarried adults aged fifty through sixty-four were living together but not married, up from 7 percent in 2000.
- From 1980 to 1998, divorce among men sixty-five and older doubled, from 5 to 10 percent. Among women sixty-five and older, it tripled, from 4 to 12 percent.
- In 2010 one out of every twenty people in the United States who got divorced was sixty-five or older. The baby boomers—fifty to sixty-four—divorced at more than four times that rate.[2]

According to the Pew Research Center, for the first time in the modern era living with a parent or parents is edging out other living arrangements for eighteen- to thirty-four-year-olds. As of 2014, slightly more than 31 percent of Millennials were living with parents, slightly more than the percentage living with a life partner or cohabiting. Of the rest, 14 percent lived with family other than their parents or in group residences, like college dorms, and 14 percent lived independently—as a single parent, with roommates, or alone.[3]

WHERE TO GO NEXT

Part of manning up to the changes aging brings is being clear-eyed about *where* home will be. "Where" may depend on "whether." Whether you're alone or with a partner. Whether you have an aging parent (or both), or you're becoming the aging parent trying to decide whether your presence is regarded by your children as a gift or a burden. Whether you have a support network where you are or never really formed one. Whether you have been prudent in financial affairs or find you need help.

Assessing an approaching senior landscape is an ongoing process for some of the foresighted men among us, starting before change becomes imminent. They have long-term health-care policies in place (cheaper when you're younger, possible to age out of if you wait long enough). They have a specific destination and warmer climate in mind, or they have aging-in-place plans that include intergenerational volunteer and civic activities they may already have begun to cultivate. They may have family far away who need and want them nearby and so elect to move away from the area and home that has been familiar all their lives. They may recognize early a preference for life in a community that is restricted to people fifty-five and older, as **David W.** does in Kissimmee, Florida. He likes the quieter atmosphere of an adult community with only the occasional tumult visiting children and grandchildren bring. He also likes the security of community services in the forms of property maintenance and safety that his senior community, like most, provides.

For others, the need for adjustments feels abrupt, calling to mind the fable of the ant and the grasshopper. Today's senior man is most likely to be a combination of ant and grasshopper, having thought at least vaguely or perhaps seriously about the need to provide in some way for this part of life but still likely to be surprised by unforeseen circumstances and the accommodations circumstances make necessary. Fortunately, the choices and opportunities are far more possible and available than they have ever been, with distance, community, and even travel experience being redefined by Skype, the Internet, and Google.

You met **Norman C.** in chapter 5. Norman, long divorced and his children grown with families of their own, lives alone, contentedly. His busy life is very full because of his intellectual curiosity and his social life. If you were to move to Norman's neighborhood, you wouldn't need a guidebook; Norman knows everything anyone would need to know about it.

> *I can't know everything, of course, but I make it my business to know my city—its politics, its museums, and everything I need to know about. I never run out of things that interest me. As a senior, I have so much available to me. Once I started at the senior center where we met, I found another one that had other activities I like, too, so I go to both. I always really loved school, and when I found out I could go*

back to college, not have to pay for it or take exams, I just couldn't believe my luck. The buses are free at my age. I still see family and people I've known for years at church. It's actually costing me less than I expected to do things I really love to do. Just ask me about anything that's available to seniors—I'm an expert!

CAUTIONARY TALES

Solitude is fine, but you need someone to tell that solitude is fine.
—Honoré de Balzac

There is a vast difference between being alone and being lonely. As shown in the Pew statistics above, the numbers of people living alone has increased dramatically just in the past twenty years, and the trend is definitely on the upswing. But just because living alone has lost its social stigma and is no longer viewed negatively doesn't mean it will necessarily fit you as a way of life.

Both **Mark S.** and **Herbert G.**—each vigorous and active in their nineties—had long marriages. Mark and his wife met as children:

My wife and I grew up together, starting when we were eight years old. We were married for sixty-four years. I am not looking for another relationship. I have no interest in meeting anyone.

When Mark says "anyone," he doesn't mean that he does not enjoy the company of others and actively seek it out. He means another person with whom to share his life exclusively.

Herbert says that he loves the company of others and has a special friendship with a woman who shares his love of theater and music, but living alone in his own space is what he prefers.

By contrast, there is **Leonard F.** of Newton, Massachusetts, whose marriage to Sweetie (she had another name, but no one ever heard her called anything else) always seemed to be of the classic wished-for variety: romantic and devoted from their late teens on. She supported him through professional school and ran his home and legal office. They raised their children and faced attendant ups and downs together, including her last protracted illness. She stuck by him through professional difficulties that nearly led to Len's disbarment after he was implicated in a scandal involving roofers in Boston. In their late sixties, when their three children were grown and living mostly at a distance, they downsized, sold their house, and moved to a large condominium building. At sixty-eight, Sweetie died. Her family followed the Jewish tradition of shiva, the seven-day mourning period during which friends and relatives visit the bereaved. One of Len's neighbors in the building told her divorced friend, Karen, about the newly eligible man in the next wing. Karen had never actually met Len or Sweetie herself. Invited by her friend to come along for a shiva visit, Karen prepared a delicious and apparently truly tempting casserole. And the rest is history. Len's second (Karen's third) marriage took place a few months later, with unfortunate consequences, including alienation of Len's children and the loss of most of his network of friends. In his own words:

I think I really was afraid to be alone. I really never had been on my own. I lived at home when I went to college, couldn't afford the dorm. Then the army. Then we got married, and I went to law school while my wife taught school. In the last few years I was taking care of Sweetie full-time, when she was ill. We were always totally wrapped up in each other—even, I think, to the exclusion of our kids sometimes. I realize she was still really supporting me emotionally. I should have given myself a chance to adjust to being without her. When I met Karen, the differences [from Sweetie] that I found interesting and exciting at first pretty soon became very hard for me to live with.

Now, I'm living in the bigger-than-I-needed-or-wanted house, newly built near the condo. We moved here to have room for her mother, who died soon after, and Karen's dog—who was barred from the condo building after her first dog, who'd been grandfathered in—died. We split. She moved away. Staying in the house was the easiest thing to do. I provide room and board for a man who helps me and cooks and is here at night in case of emergencies.

I'm surprised that I don't feel lonely. Maybe because I have the security that knowing someone is in the house helps. I still visit some old friends in the condo building where I used to live, or I call and visit on the phone. I'm able to keep myself amused. It's wonderful to have the computer and movies I can watch any time. I really find I need company less and less. I'm also relieved.

Leonard's story is an example of the hazards of making important decisions when we're most vulnerable and least capable of weighing pros and cons rationally.

Ronnie G. of Ambler, Pennsylvania, seventy-four, thought he had figured out what to do very carefully. An accountant, he definitely has the skills and experience necessary to make good financial decisions, but here is what actually happened:

> *I was seventy-one when Susan, my wife, died. We had what I can only describe as an excellent marriage. Our kids live far away, but I still have friends and activities I care about here. I found it painful to stay in the home we had built together. I appreciated my children's invitations to move—to Denver or to Los Angeles—but I really didn't want to. Several places near me have good reputations as retirement communities I could definitely afford, and I picked one that keeps me close to old friends and activities I like. So I sold the house six months later and moved. It's fine, but I'm finding that the overall [corporate] ownership of the residence has changed, and the new owners are raising the cost of living here appreciably. It's a nice place, and I could manage, but I'm thinking it's not a good idea to stay.*

What's going into your decision?

> *I'm thinking that the new cost won't really be worth it. Besides, I'm angry—I feel blindsided by the change I couldn't foresee, especially, I guess, because I'm an accountant and I'm not feeling I can count on my contract with this place. What if this company sells the property to Trump?? Then what might happen?*

> *I'm still in good health, but I'm aware that some of my friends are not, and I'm wondering if being here is still best for me. I feel that the extra money living here will cramp my style of living somewhat—make me more reluctant to pick up and fly out to Denver and LA so often. I'm certainly not making this decision in haste, but it is a painful one. I've signaled my kids to start scouting their areas for possible alternatives.*

Ronnie's dilemma is not unusual. It is complicated by his initial too-precipitous decision to sell the home he and his wife had built together so soon after her death. Perhaps even living elsewhere temporarily would have helped him reach the decision to sell and commit to a new living place less emotionally. And the example of finding that the initial contract with a new residence is less binding than expected is, alas, not unusual. Even accountants may not be ready to sign up when grief is governing emotions. Most experts advise waiting a year or more.

ALONE OR LONELY

The difference between solitude and loneliness is enormous. More people in the United States live alone than ever, and this trend will continue as more and more Millennials put off marriage or never marry. Of those who do, it isn't clear how many do by choice and how many are left alone by the circumstance of divorce or death of a partner. For those in the latter group, it is also unclear how many wish they were living with someone else. Now, about one-third of Americans older than sixty-five live alone, and half of those over eighty-five do. Dr. Dhruv Khullar reported in the *New York Times* on the growing epidemic of social isolation, which brings with it dire physical, mental, and emotional consequences. Since the 1980s, Dr. Khullar found, the percentage of American adults who say they're lonely doubled from 20 percent to 40 percent. Loneliness can accelerate cognitive decline in older adults, and premature death is twice as likely among isolated individuals as those with robust social interactions. A recent study found that isolation increases the risk of heart disease by 29 percent and stroke by 32 percent. In all, loneliness is found to be as important a risk factor for early death as obesity and smoking. [4]

FACING LONELINESS

What is clear, however, is that a man living alone does not necessarily signal loneliness. It is possible to feel lonely in a crowd or in a relationship of two people. Not being lonely means you have found kindred spirits and connections outside yourself. Loneliness, as shown in research, can be toxic, particularly when it is experienced along with social isolation. For the person living alone by choice, however, it's important to recognize signs of withdrawal from social contact. Maintaining friendships and activities that bring you in contact with people on a regular basis is vital to maintaining mental and emotional health, whether you're living alone or not.

A study at the University of California–San Francisco followed 1,600 adults with an average age of seventy-one. Nearly 23 percent of lonely participants died within six years of the study as opposed to 14 percent of those who reported adequate companionship. The study controlled for socioeconomic status and health, so we may conclude that loneliness was the life-shortening factor.[5]

A DEALING-WITH-LONELINESS HOW-TO

For some men, admitting to feeling lonely is definitely "anti–manning up." It's an admission of weakness. If you feel lonely, remember that it's a virtually universal experience, but if it persists and becomes hard to bear, it's a danger signal. Should that happen to you, *don't let it slide without taking steps.* The way out and forward is easier than you might realize.

- For people connected to religious institutions, continuing to attend services and events is a resource not only for spiritual balm but also for social connection, a feeling of community, and a possible place for volunteering.
- Adopting a pet is no trivial pursuit. It forces the care of something other than oneself while bringing the pleasure of the nonjudgmental affection an animal can offer. Try the animal shelter in your town; somebody there needs you. You may wind up not only with a four-legged pal but with a great volunteering opportunity to boot.
- Check out local colleges and universities. Most have opportunities for seniors to audit courses at no or low cost. Just being in the atmosphere and interacting with younger people—and learning—is invigorating.
- Think of Norman C. and find a line-dancing class at a senior center. It's something you do alone yet in a group and is easy, pleasurable exercise, and you can't help feeling a relaxed group vibe.
- Meditate mindfully. Learn the difference between rumination (consciously dwelling on negative events and feelings) and meditation. Practice!
- Yoga.
- Move.

DID WE JUST SAY "MOVE"??

You read it correctly. Although the vast majority of seniors and those anticipating retirement express a definite preference to remain in their own homes, or perhaps move to another single-dwelling place, for a growing number it is a really good, if difficult, decision to move into senior housing rather than remaining to "age in place." In your grandparents' and even your parents' day, moving to a "retirement place" was considered tantamount to entering a nursing home—definitely conjuring the idea immediately of "the end of the line." And we don't mean the conga line.

Here's Thelma again:

> *I remember vividly my Aunt Sallie who entered the Home for the Aged in her late seventies; when I visited her, she said, "If you visit again and they tell you I'm on the fourth floor, don't bother to come up!" Ever the purveyor of mordant wit, Sallie's standard answer to "How are you?" had always been "Lousy, thank you."*

Today there are various types of living arrangements and communities that fall under the general heading of senior housing, most of which have their qualifying age as low as fifty-five. They range from apartment buildings that are simply age-restricted to planned retirement communities that are designed for active older adults. (See all those smiling, biking, tennis-playing, romantic, youthful-but-gray-haired people on television.) They range in price from "only the wealthy need apply" to middle-class affordable to attainable to those on a limited, fixed income. AARP research tells us that nearly 90 percent of seniors want to stay in their own homes as they age ("aging in place"), some of whom do make adaptations to their homes to accommodate physical changes. These include installing grab bars in bathrooms and higher electrical outlets, modifying entrances to the house to get rid of steps, and replacing slippery floor surfaces. Relatively few of these seniors remaining in their own homes (14 percent) expect to require day-to-day assistance or ongoing health care at any point during their retirement. However, statistics about the likelihood of living independently change when the questions are put to the adult children of aging parents. More than half the children think their parents will need their help, while less than three in ten older parents agree.[6] It may be time for a serious talk with family!

AGING IN PLACE PLUS

Aging in place has taken on new meaning for over six hundred diverse seniors in Philadelphia. A group called Friends in the City—FitC— started several years ago when four couples who liked being in the center of town organized a book club and a walking group. They wanted to expand their activities to take advantage of their location, its resources, and the opportunities for mutual support and volunteer activities. The "friends" in their name is ambiguous, referring to the relationship of members and to the Religious Society of Friends (Quakers). It is now a nonprofit organization operating under the aegis of the Friends Center City Retirement Community and has received grants from the Friends Foundation for the Aging for their loosely knit urban continuous-care retirement community.[7] Any group receiving funds from the foundation is open to all and operates in accordance with Quaker practices.

FitC activities are organized by and for members and include health and fitness, cultural, educational, creative, volunteer, and dining-group occasions. Membership costs $70 per year. Programs include music, film and book discussions, foreign-language practice groups, current-events lunches, photography exhibitions, and writing groups. They have expanded to create a residential condo building called Friends Center City–Riverfront (available only to those who have Friends Life Care or equivalent long-term-care insurance); a concierge service, FitC PLUS; and an aging-in-place health-care plan, Friends Life Care, a national Quaker-inspired organization.

Whether "Friends" is spelled with a capital "F" for Quaker or a small "f" for non-Quaker, Friends in the City appears to be working brilliantly as hundreds of members, diverse in every way, including age (mostly seniors), experience "what people want more than anything else," according to one member: community.

ONE KIND OF NEW HOME

Eric M., seventy-five, of Riverdale, New York, has lived alone in subsidized senior housing for ten years. He is qualified by age and disability for housing well within his modest means. His studio apartment is neat and well cared for, as is the building. He described the advantages of living there:

> One of the best things about this place is the location. I can walk to everything I need, even a movie theater. And I know just about everybody here. Sometimes I help out and work at the desk in the lobby, which I like. Most of the people here are women. They're really nice. I cook for myself mostly, but someone always invites me for dinner or gives me cake or cookies when they bake. It's a win-win—they like to feed someone, and I like to eat!

We met **Alvin C.**, seventy-three, on the sunny terrace of the senior housing complex in Philadelphia, Pennsylvania, that has been his home for the past four years. Over tea, he told us his story:

> I retired from my work at the postal service when I was sixty-five. At that time my wife had already retired from her job at a preschool. We had a good life and lived in our own home until she became ill. We managed together and with the assistance of our daughters until my wife passed four years ago. Both of my daughters wanted me to come and live with them and their families. I really appreciated that, and it was very hard for them, too; they lost their mother. I tried it for a while. But I really wasn't happy. As much as I love them and my grandkids, I really couldn't get used to feeling I just wasn't on my own anymore. They were all great, and I didn't want to hurt their feelings, but I realized I just wasn't ready to feel that the role of aging dad and grandpop was my whole identity now.

> One of my old friends from the post office moved here and kept telling me how much he likes it. He's also on his own now. I liked his apartment—it had everything I'd need, including a nice little well-equipped kitchen. I could even arrange to rent a parking space for my car less than a block away until a free space becomes available here. The rent is really reasonable, and I definitely made the right move.

What are the things you like best about living here?

> I really like being among other retired people who are still active, and that's most of the people I know here. There's a group I found that I play cards with and some I watch football with. Sometimes we get together in someone's apartment or in the community room. I'm definitely never lonesome. We have a small library—everybody turns in

books they finished reading and can take out new ones. I can take walks in the neighborhood or drive to my kids' houses or the hospital where I do volunteer work. I like the security of the place, too. I'm still in the city, but I don't have to worry about safety when I'm here. And I am more relaxed about money. I am able to live within my income and not rely on my savings. I don't have to call the roofer or the plumber anymore to fix my house or replace old appliances. That definitely feels good!

Are there planned activities?

No. Once in a while we have a visiting choral group, which is nice, or someone who comes and gives a talk, but we're on our own for entertainment, which is fine with me. I still go out to movies or for dinner sometimes. Eating is easy at home with the microwave or cooking for myself. I always have a jigsaw puzzle set up on a card table in my living room—for myself and anybody else who comes in, especially my grandkids. It gives us something to do together.

Alvin appreciated the support of his children when his wife died, and the fact that they wanted him to live with them was reassuring. But he came to the realization that moving in with family felt wrong for him. It represented entering a stage of life he wasn't ready for—perhaps, he felt, a diminishment of his independence. He knew himself well enough to make the decision.

ANOTHER KIND

On a very personal note, one of the by-products that accompanies the publishing of a successful book (*The New Senior Woman*) is the opportunity and privilege to travel, visit, and speak in many venues. One of those visits remains especially vivid—only in part because the temperature on that February day was eight degrees Fahrenheit. The warmth of the atmosphere at St. John's in Rochester, New York, more than compensated for the icy outdoors. And while we never suggest actually moving anywhere without seriously checking out every last nook and cranny of the place you're considering, and checking every jot and tittle of the legalities involved, my immediate feeling was "What a wonderful place!"—a feeling that was borne out by much I learned since that initial impression. Impressive, to me, was the fact that, while St. John's is large and self-contained, it doesn't feel or act that way in its integration into the larger community of city, university, and all of the diversity, including age and cultural advantages that brings.

I contacted one of the administrators I had met, who referred me to one of the active residents who agreed to a telephone interview.

Dick Gollin has been retired as professor emeritus in the English department of the University of Rochester for twenty-five years; his wife, Rita K. Gollin, retired as distinguished professor emerita from SUNY–Geneseo. They've been married for sixty-seven years. (Since they were twenty-two. That's right: they are both eighty-nine.) Dick has taught at the University of Minnesota, Colgate, and Rochester, was a Fulbright scholar at Oxford and the recipient of many grants, and has served on many distinguished councils and panels. Immersed for many years in the study and teaching of Victorian literature and intellectual history, he focused particularly on Matthew Arnold and Arthur Hugh Clough. Eventually, and notably, Dick introduced film studies at the University of Rochester and wrote *A Viewer's Guide to Film: Arts, Artifices, and Issues.*[8]

> *We met as students at Queens College and went on to graduate school together at the University of Minnesota. Our three children are scattered around the country, and when Rita got very seriously ill several years ago they signed us in here, assuming we would be safer, more secure. It seems we spend the first twenty or thirty years worrying about our children and the last decade having them worry about us. She recovered, but by then our knees had begun to give way, and we decided to stay on—first in an apartment, then in a bungalow when one became available.[9] We moved from a three-story house we had lived in for forty-four years. We each brought several cartons of partly written things—part of the world of good intentions—that remain stored in our garage. Perhaps it's part of realizing that at our age we can disengage and watch the spectacle.*

How is living here working out for you?

> *We don't make much use of the activities here; we still keep up with our life before moving here. The biggest advantage is that assistance is regularly and readily available should we need it. About half our furniture is now in about a third or a quarter of the space, so wherever we walk there's immediately a wall or a piece of furniture to brace on.*

Having very little open space is an advantage now. Should we need it, there is the slow adaptation from independent living to assisted living to nursing care here. I still drive and walk with two canes. I used to ski, but I find that my joints and knees no longer tolerate it. But I noticed that when I go for longer walks with two canes I have a cross-country stride!

Stride is the operative word here: Dick and his wife seem to be taking the challenges that come with aging in stride. Should they find the furniture, the garage, and the cooking more than they can handle or want, transitions to lifestyle changes are relatively smooth where they are now.

Both Alvin and Dick have found that aging in place was not ideal for them and have found places that suit their needs and financial circumstances. The availability and range of accommodations for senior living is very wide—and so are the costs. Adequate, comfortable housing is available at costs within quite limited, fixed incomes, as is high-end, luxury living in continuous-care communities. It takes a well-educated consumer at any stage of the spectrum to decide wisely, as well as research beyond word-of-mouth or surface observation. The research should always include how costs are maintained versus at what rate they may escalate.

Age discrimination is allowed in senior housing—it's perfectly legal to operate a fifty-five-plus property. The 1968 Fair Housing Act protects home buyers and renters from discrimination based on seven different areas: race, color, sex, national origin, religion, familial status, and disability. Many states have additional laws protecting such classes as marital status, sexual orientation, and ancestry. There are often positive or negative "vibes," however, that are worth checking out before making any commitment. What sometimes lurk beneath the surface are subtle signs of discrimination, particularly as reported among LGBTQ seniors who recognize some communities as definitely unwelcoming. *The brochure never tells everything you need to know.* We remember vividly the nonagenarian woman Hanne Jonas, widow of philosopher Hans Jonas, at a premier senior residence who longed for more intellectually stimulating activities and told us for *The New Senior Woman*, "It's hard for me to get out. I read a lot, but any book discussion group here stops at best-selling fiction!" Unfortunately, that was the one attribute that had been taken for granted without investigation when her daughter searched for senior communities for her mom.

Many places have very stimulating discussion groups, like the one **Irving R.** attends. (See more of Irving's story in chapters 3 and 8.) Others have a strong focus on the arts. At one of our local Positive Aging group lunch meetings, one man who had recently moved into a fairly modest retirement community was anxious to tell me that after all those years of teaching math and thinking of himself as "strictly a numbers guy," he had become a poet after taking a poetry workshop offered at his new residence. Writing every day, he said, has given him a whole new interest in reading and a new perspective on life—and on himself. "It feels like a new me!" he said. Other places have facilities that awaken hitherto undeveloped passions for painting, sculpture, and jewelry making. All still have larger percentages of women than men, but the odds are shrinking as men's longevity catches up to that of women. Needless to say, unattached men are very popular, especially those who never before realized how attractive to women they could be and—bonus—are still able to drive.

We admit we haven't met any of the rare men (or women) who are spending retirement years on the high seas—but it may be fun to think about. Such an idea is not merely an urban legend but actually exists in reality. Staying on a cruise ship apparently costs only about $2,000 more than the cost of assisted living, which is about $229 daily for a private room in a nursing home and $3,293 per month for a one-bedroom residence in an assisted-living facility, according to LongTermCare.gov. [10] These figures, often cited by cruise-ship companies and travel advisors, are somewhat misleading, however, as it is unlikely that someone planning a lengthy cruise is in need of assisted living. He is much more likely to be a vigorous retiree still living independently in his life on land.

A six-month around-the-world cruise, starting at about $40,000, has been on offer at Oceania Cruises, enabling a couple (same price for one or two together) to have laundry and Internet service, onboard medical care, and fine dining included. Healthy people who live in expensive locales, and who have the means, may find that moving to more inexpensive homes on land and living part of the year at sea is a money-saving venture. According to the Cruise Lines International Association, more people are cruising now than ever before, with twenty-four million passengers expected to cruise in 2017 compared with fifteen million ten years ago. About a quarter of those are sixty to seventy-four years old, and another quarter are ages fifty to fifty-nine. Cruise ships offer housekeeping services, entertainment, and, often, educational programs, such as onboard lecture series. A fitness center, library, swimming pool, and twenty-four-hour meal service are usually standard features. No one includes the price of shopping in all those exotic ports of call, however, so come prepared. If you're interested, book early; six-month cruise accommodations have wait-lists a year or more in advance.

At the pinnacle of life-at-sea possibilities is becoming one of the 165 homeowners of *The World*, the largest private residential ship on the planet. The environmentally friendly *World* first launched in 2002, continuously circumnavigating the globe. The passengers (residents) are from about forty countries and luxuriate in apartments ranging from studios to three-bedroom suites, all with ever-changing sea views and teak verandas. It's possible to rent or provide time onboard as a gift to friends for weeks during the year, but firsthand reviews suggest that temporary travelers often feel snubbed by regulars. Keep that in mind before you go.

We were unable to interview any men who cruise the world—on the oceans—perpetually.

Home can be anywhere you make it. Make it comfortable. Make it a haven. Leave it frequently, but always come back.

7

HEALTH, SEX, AND INTIMACY

Give me health and a day, and I will make the pomp of emperors ridiculous.

—Ralph Waldo Emerson, *Nature*

WHAT DO WE MEAN BY "HEALTH," ANYWAY?

The view changes; the prism shifts. For most men, what good health is suddenly is made manifest when it's no longer there. There is no arguing, no matter what the latest "discoveries" touted by commercial (usually unregulated) health and fitness companies say: physical aging happens, accompanied by changes most men did not consciously expect. That was probably a good thing when, except for serious athletes, energy and focus were given to other facts and aspects of life. But with the first aches and twinges, or other reminders that adjustments will have to be made, awareness creeps in or pops up with the force of a sledgehammer. The sensible man has a qualified doctor he trusts, and if he doesn't, he finds another. He's paying attention without becoming obsessed or failing to make adjustments in his activities or routine that make sense. He recognizes that mental, emotional, and even spiritual health are inextricably tied to the optimal functioning of his physical body.

MANNING UP TO TAKING CONTROL

Before publishing experts prevailed, we wanted to call *The New Senior Woman*, our first book, *Mastering the Art of a Senior Life*. As we explained, "The science is up to our doctors; the art is up to us." So much of what happens to our aging bodies cannot be foreseen or forestalled. The art, and our control, lies in prevention, mental and physical fitness, emotional response, and attitude. Blessed with good health, men you've met here, like **Alan G.**, of Chappaqua, New York, and **John Santa**, continue to exercise vigorously (organized games for Alan or skiing for John). **Oliver Franklin** and **Peter H.** are still at the gym every morning, recognizing that "keeping up" with the younger men is not the goal—their own fitness is the point. **Tom L.**, now walking regularly along Wissahickon Creek, decries the stress he witnesses as older men strain to run when walking might serve them better now. **Norman C.** finds that line dancing at one of the senior centers he attends is exercise he enjoys and contributes to his social as well as his physical well-being.

Unpreventable, unexpected illness or injuries present tests of more than physical strength. **Dada** reminds us that "there is a big difference between pain and suffering." The discipline he follows of devotional meditation and routine, he says, "keeps my mind off my body." Rather than give up his daily walk, he adapts to change by using a walker. **John Creveling** says, "Parkinson's disease doesn't define me," and he gives evidence of that determination in the richness of his life and activities. Both of these men exhibit great inner strength, and both have the advantage of support—Dada living in a spiritual community and with close family members near at hand, and John with a devoted partner in his wife. Both recognize their good fortune in having that support, in not going it alone.

You met **Irving R.** in chapter 3, the centenarian scientist. His serious vision and hearing impairments do not keep him from continuing to expand and share his knowledge:

> *I find that using an iPad is great because I am able to enlarge print and spacing of material as I read. As for my hearing loss, I must say my ability to read facial expressions and body language has gotten really good, enhancing communication for me. I get a great deal of pleasure in sharing knowledge, as I did when you heard my lecture on Einstein, although Q and A sessions require good equipment—micro-*

phones—and someone to make sure the audience members and I clear-ly get each other's meaning. Taking care of interesting plants requires no hearing and no more vision than is readily available to me. And I love doing that. Botany remains an interest I pursue.

I visited Irving at his home in an assisted-living community and learned something about how he handles his sensory limitations.

I have two major difficulties: I am legally blind, and I'm hard of hearing. So my means of communicating with others is very limited.

You are obviously very involved in the world, and you tend to reach out rather than be self-absorbed. How do you keep in touch and get your information?

I had to give up my computer because I could not magnify the images large enough. That was a terrible loss for me. However, I now have a TV adapter than enables me to adjust the light and size of print of anything from a cereal box to The Economist, *the* Scientific American, *and* National Geographic, *all of which I subscribe to. I have to read slowly, because it takes a long time for the print to register on my retina. This is enormously important to me.*

Tonight we have a discussion group that meets every two weeks. We talk about current events, music, arts, theology, biology, et cetera. When the group—or any group—gets together, I have particular trou-ble with background. But I have this little mic than can be passed around. When someone talks, he holds it, and I can hear him clear as a bell. Without it I'd be completely isolated.

Irving refuses to let his physical limitations limit his engagement with others and the intellectual stimulation and satisfaction that enable him to thrive at one hundred.

GOING IT ALONE

In chapter 5 we dealt with other effects of loneliness, but it deserves consideration in any discussion of physical needs as men age as well. Research in the past twenty years in both the United States and the United Kingdom suggests that loneliness has become a public-health issue that merits greater attention as the population ages.[1] The effects of loneliness are being measured not only in psychological or sociological terms but also in physical or medical terms. Chronic loneliness apparently can seriously affect blood pressure and the production of white blood cells and can result in the impairment of the immune system's ability to fight infections. When **Mark S.**, at ninety-two, tells us that his friends "keep him going," he isn't kidding! It's very likely that the decision he made to develop his contacts with others and give them the pleasure of his company is as vital to his physical health as it is to his renewed enjoyment of living.

THE "D" WORD

Manning up does not mean assuming that sadness or depression will just go away if you don't talk about it. Recognize that the emotional toll taken by depression is an aspect of mental health that affects physical health. A macho "Get over it!" attitude can serve you well and probably has. Nevertheless, reaching this stage of maturity means you have by now been through some crises where that attitude may not have been enough. A serious news event, loss of loved ones or of capabilities through physical injuries, changes of job or status, or the trauma of separation or divorce can all trigger deep sadness or even depression. Usually we can pinpoint the trigger for sadness, but sometimes depression occurs without an obvious cause. It's important to know the difference.

Periods of sadness can still be relieved by some enjoyment of things you care about in normal time—music, a movie, a visit with friends or family. Distraction is possible, and the distractions offer the promise of eventual release from the oppressive feeling of gloom. But what if the distractions never seem to work, the sadness persists or deepens, and other signs appear? If sleep patterns change, appetite is seriously affected, or thoughts of self-harm are present, toughing it out is usually unwise and always unnecessary. If personal confidences make you uncomfortable, keep the subject professional and check in with your physician, who can refer you to a mental-health professional for help. The Anxiety and Depression Association of America has a list of online resources for depression that anyone can use to find licensed professionals in any area of the country.[2]

THE "A" WORD

Remember that joke back in chapter 1—the one about the guy in his pajamas who's sitting on the side of the bed and can't remember whether he's about to go to sleep or get up for the day? It may not be so funny if you're worried about memory loss and not sure why it's happening. The fear is often overwhelming, especially in men who have witnessed Alzheimer's onset in a parent, spouse, or friend. **Perry H.** of Austin, Texas, a sixty-year-old practicing attorney, told us,

> *I was so worried about forgetting so much I called my doctor after doing my usual Googling about "conditions." I was sure it was early-onset Alzheimer's. He sent me to the university for tests. Turned out I'm perfectly normal. Or so they say. I definitely am getting worse at names and need to make notes and lists more than I used to. It's a good thing the beeper on the gizmo tells me where I parked the car, too; otherwise, I'd wind up walking around the whole block! And since when is it normal to call the cat my wife's name and vice versa?*

Well, okay, Perry. You probably will have to start making lists and notes more regularly. And be grateful for the beeper that tells you where you parked. (Just don't forget to take the gizmo with you!) By the way, keep doing the crossword puzzles you've always loved—Sudoku, too. Good exercise for the little gray cells. And try to relax, although that may be contrary to your nature. Anxiety may be interfering with your memory a bit. Incidentally, recent research suggests that ballroom dancing may be even more beneficial to mental alertness than crossword puzzles!

Perry was smart. He didn't just dwell on an awful prospect; he did something about it by consulting his doctor. Real concerns are nothing to sneeze at.

THE "P" WORD

P is for *prostate*. The American Cancer Society tells us that about one man in seven will be diagnosed with prostate cancer during his lifetime.[3] The good news is that most men diagnosed with prostate cancer will not die from it but will still be living with it at the end of life. The not-so-good news is that most symptoms do not appear until the cancer has progressed beyond the optimum time for diagnosis. If you're old enough to find this book interesting, you're old enough to talk to your doctor about screening for prostate cancer. This is a confusing area, as guidelines for screening and treatment are constantly changing.

A VISION OF AGING

Dr. **Joseph Maroon**, of the University of Pittsburgh Medical Center, is professor, researcher, author, neurosurgeon, health and fitness expert, Ironman triathlete, and team neurosurgeon for the Pittsburgh Steelers. Still at the top of his game professionally in his seventies, Joseph shared his vision of aging with us in an article he was writing for the *Pittsburgh Tribune*:

> *Dr. Perry Gresham, former president of Bethany College, succinctly and eloquently portrayed human aging best in his book,* With Wings as Eagles.[4] *He described two commonly held aging analogies and then proposed an alternative approach that provides hope and purpose as we age. The first equates human aging to an automobile. Many, especially physicians, hold to this analogy. Like a car, our bodies, over time, gradually deteriorate, fail mechanically despite various operations, replacement parts, and repairs and eventually wind up in the scrap heap—a.k.a. the funeral parlor. This analogy holds out little hope or expectation of a better future and exemplifies the theory of entropy: all material things eventually decline, degrade, and collapse.*
>
> *The second image dating back thousands of years is that of a tree or vegetation that changes with the seasons. There is initially youth in the springtime, maturity in summer, old age in autumn, and death in winter. Again, this organic determinism is just as fatalistic as mechanical determinism. This analogy also describes a preordained, unwavering decline that is inevitable. Might there be a less pessimistic or better aging analogy or mode? Dr. Gresham thinks so. In his sixties, he experienced a new burst of energy and creativity best described as "regeneration" of both body and mind. I, too, starting in my sixties have had a similar renewal. Rather than the inexorable degradation with aging, implicit in the car and tree analogies, I have experienced a period of* renewed vitality *even though I am, at times, painfully conscious of my own aging and ongoing entropy!*

This renewal phenomenon was actually described over 2,700 years ago by the prophet Isaiah when he wrote, "But they that wait upon the Lord shall renew their strength; *they shall mount up with wings as eagles; they shall run and not be weary; and they shall walk and not faint" (Isaiah 40:31). Dr. Gresham referred to this late-life renewal as the "eagle-wing aging theory."*

Ironically, for many years this verse was a mantra for me to suppress pain and fatigue during athletic endurance like the Ironman triathlon in Kona, Hawaii. I desperately wanted to "run and not be weary and walk and not be faint"! It was in my early sixties, however, when I finally appreciated what Isaiah additionally meant by "renewed strength." Life can *be a series of "renewals" rather than irreversible decline even in the sixties and seventies! I discovered that "to wait upon the Lord" simply means, as best we can, to do the "right thing" at the right time—morally, physically, and spiritually. Embracing religion, meditation, a strong family unit or a set of guiding principles can reduce stress and thereby improve longevity and mitigate many of the chronic diseases associated with aging. Regular exercise prolongs healthy longevity and also prevents common diseases like diabetes, heart disease, and cognitive decline. It also is the most effective antidepressant! Finally, it means to avoid excess in all things.*

There are those like Ponce de León who search incessantly for the fountain or elixir of youth but are doomed to failure. By subscribing to the eagle's-wing theory, I truly have experienced the "renewal" described by Isaiah. I continue to find new projects, challenges, and commitments, both in and outside of medicine, and cultivate stimulating friendships. The good news is you too can choose a healthy diet, commit to regular exercise, and better manage stress through prayer, meditation, yoga, et cetera, in order to have the best chance at a longer, healthier life. Search for the renewal and creativity within oneself, make better choices now, and strive to do what is "right"!

I am not delusional about the oncoming day of my final exit or when the various diseases I confront daily in my neurosurgical practice may suddenly strike and "breath becomes air." Unexpectedly in the fourth quarter, however, I am more creative, more empathetic, and enjoying life more than any time before. I am reaping the fruits of lifestyle choices made early on and with renewed strength and wings as eagles find neurosurgery and my relationships more fulfilling than ever.

Think of **Dick Gollin**, in chapter 6, whose two-cane long-walk stride reminds him of the cross-country skiing no longer in his range of physical exercise, or of Dada, in chapter 2, who adapts to physical changes in inspiring ways and reminds us of "the difference between pain and suffering." And be sure to check in again with Irving R., in chapter 3, who at one hundred, though legally blind and extremely hard of hearing, continues to find ways to adapt to sensory changes, to lecture, to participate in stimulating discussion, and to study. They are not deniers—of age or encroaching infirmity. They are surely examples of manning up and more: their lives are full.

CAVEAT EMPTOR

Dr. Maroon's observation that those who search incessantly for the fountain or elixir of youth are doomed to failure is worth repeating and thinking about. How vulnerable are you to the barrage of advertisements that flood every means of communication in your life? What is the latest imperfection or sign of diminishment you've been reminded of today? And what miracles of youthful looks, vigor, and sexual performance are being promised with the press of a key on your computer, the submission of your credit card number, or visit to your local vitamin, health, and nutritional-supplements store? We're not saying that you may not find useful products there or online. What we are saying is: *buyer, beware* (or, once again, *caveat emptor*, for Latin lovers). From home testing (IVD—in vitro diagnostic) products that promise to diagnose HIV (or measure your cholesterol) to hair and libido restorers, from capsules promising to increase penis size to nostrums that will help you sleep like a baby (not the baby who wakes up every three hours and cries), you will find them all on TV or popping up on the Internet. Some have websites that will knock your socks off. Never let the website fool you. Wonderful Web designers abound. You still have to read the fine print and use your head, balding or not. Remember, you're in control here, not the marketplace. Here are some guidelines to follow when you're at your local drugstore or checking out products on the Web:

- Most IVD tests should be followed by a second, more sophisticated, lab test, available through your doctor. The results you get at home are not definitive or even reliable necessarily.
- Tests advertised for determining the presence of drugs such as marijuana, nicotine, amphetamine, and methamphetamine in children and employees are insufficient without additional lab tests.
- PSA—prostate surface antigen—tests, for prostate cancer, are for screening only and should be used in conjunction with a rectal exam performed by a doctor.
- If the product is made in a country other than the United States, check to see whether the FDA has cleared or approved the test for use at home.
- Avoid websites that do not provide a phone number.
- Don't trust websites that claim the government, medical profession, or research scientists are in cahoots to suppress their product.
- Avoid anything that claims to be a "new cure" or "miracle cure." (Where was the Nobel Prize if it really worked?)
- Avoid websites with impressive-sounding terminology that isn't backed up with clear explanations.
- Beware of claims that the test or product "complies with all regulatory agencies." Look for FDA approval.

SEX AND INTIMACY: THREE GENERATIONS, THREE VIEWPOINTS

Although more than one hundred men were interviewed for this book, not one broached the topic of sex and intimacy with us, nor did they make it comfortable for us to discuss it with them. Here is the closest we got: When explaining our book to one of the focus groups we met with, one wag riposted, "Oh, you're writing about the time between virility and senility!" Many laughs erupted; no serious comments followed. We asked, "Anyone want to talk about that?" No one did, and that ended that topic.

Perhaps it is not comfortable for men to talk about this with two women. Perhaps men of this generation are not used to talking about sex and intimacy in a serious way to other men. Maybe this is a subject in which men need to display their macho selves. Maybe they're just plain embarrassed.

Fast-forward to a visit to the Student Sexuality Information Service (SSIS) at Brandeis University, where **Elisette Weiss**, student director, was very eager to show me what this program looked like. SSIS has been an integral part of Brandeis since 1973. This is a resource run "on campus *for students and by students* that aims to cultivate a safe, sex-positive community while satisfying every Brandeisian's sexual-health needs." This includes straight, LGBTQ, and sexually inactive students. The center offers a comprehensive library, a superior quantity and quality of safe-sex products, and confidential peer-counseling services. SSIS is a haven where shame and embarrassment are discouraged and discussion, openness, and knowledge take over. Compare this to the state of Texas, which has the nation's fifth-highest birthrate among teenagers, behind Arkansas, Mississippi, Oklahoma, and New Mexico. Sex education is not required in their schools. Where it is available, abstinence is the only method taught.

Boomers have generally been more open with their children about sexual matters than have post-sixty-year-olds. They accept and often encourage their children to live together before marriage. They have been more forthcoming about sex education—both in school and at home. We only have anecdotal evidence of this phenomenon, and this generalization probably is geographically specific; boomers in the South and Southwest may not fit this mold. The interesting fact here is that discussion, information, openness, education, knowledge, and awareness, rather than fostering promiscuity and loose morals, actually have the opposite effect.

Since the people we interviewed were not prolific in their comments about their sexual lives, we spoke at length to **Terri Clark**, who is prevention services coordinator at Action Wellness in Philadelphia.[5] Terri has been working in health education, training, and facilitation for nearly twenty-five years. She is a member of Widener University's Sexuality and Aging Consortium and a certified trainer with the National Resource Center on LGBT Aging, and she serves on the American Society on Aging's leadership council of their LGBT Aging Issues Network (LAIN) constituent group. Terri is also an advisory board member of Philadelphia Corporation for Aging's PrimeTime Health committee.

ARE SEX AND INTIMACY THE SAME?

After many years of marriage or partnership, sex and intimacy have become intertwined. The hormones that raged in the early years have calmed down, and intimacy has grown to include intellectual, emotional, and spiritual qualities in addition to physical ones. Physical sex is only one way to express intimacy and often wanes as people age. Health issues may interfere with continued physical sexual activity, but penetrative sex is not the only way for partners to achieve physical satisfaction. For many, in fact, it is no longer sexual intimacy as they knew it earlier but emotional intimacy and friendship, accompanied by a hug, a hand to hold, a cheek to kiss, that is sought and that satisfies.

We asked Terri to fill us in on issues that we were unable to discuss with the men we interviewed.

Terri, a question for our population is, how do men deal with their sense of masculinity, since often genitalia do not work so well anymore, for either partner—or may work to different degrees? Have you noticed that men get depressed? What can replace orgasm?

Some of what happens is that biological processes that come with aging will affect all of us, no matter what gender or what orientation we are. When it comes to sexual health and sexual response, there are changes there too. But we don't talk about this in an open honest way. There is rarely sexual education for older adults. We have to open the conversation to provide information that's targeted for older adults. So what I like to say to folks is that you need to rethink your old sexual scripts. Your body, how it worked as a young man, is not going to work sexually like that anymore. There are lots of other ways, when you are focusing sexually, that your body will work. You need to embrace that as you get to your sixties, seventies, eighties. Don't necessarily "medicalize." Don't see that as a problem. You want to come at it in different ways to explore other parts of your body that you might find pleasurable. It's not always about penetrative intercourse. We can talk about outercourse. About intimacy. Other parts of the body can be stimulating. The importance of touch. Other ways to reach orgasm. What's the role of touch now? Your brain is the most important sex organ you have, not your penis. Your skin is your largest sex organ. So men need to reframe what they thought about as sex—redefining sex, redefining good sex. Talking about what is libido. When we're younger sometimes all we need to do is start thinking about that person we're attracted to and what we'd like to do with that person turns us on. As we get older, you have to be more planful. We have to think about setting time aside to be intimate, to find pleasure with our partner or ourselves, and the mood kind of kicks in. Before, the mood was there, and then we acted on that. Now we need to redo that equation. We need to create the mood, and then the libido will get there.

Men don't talk about these issues in the same way women do. And that fits into all the relational things that women are willing to talk about. Women talk about menopause; men don't talk about andropause. Most men probably never even heard of that. They don't know what it means.

Author's Note: Andropause is also called "male menopause." It describes a drop in testosterone levels that many men experience when they get older. Declining testosterone levels can cause many symptoms. For example, it can cause depression, reduced muscle mass, increased body fat, and erectile dysfunction.

DOES ONE SIZE FIT ALL?

Of course not. It rarely does—about anything. Each man and each partnership has to find his own expressions of intimacy. The trick is to not get caught in the imbroglio of being too embarrassed to seek help. Your doctor is a huge resource, and if he or she fails to approach you about the subject, don't let that keep you from getting the information you need. Here is your chance to teach your doctor that age is no barrier to a healthy sex life.

Erectile dysfunction is perhaps the most common problem among men. Roughly 60 percent of men past sixty and 70 percent of men in their seventies have difficulty maintaining erections. So many men have prostate cancer, cardiovascular disease, or diabetes, and these are only three of the conditions that lead to erectile dysfunction. But many men and women wish to and are able to remain sexually active past eighty, needing only some support and advice, which is readily available if only they are willing to seek help.

MANAGING DIFFERENT EXPECTATIONS WITHIN A PARTNERSHIP

The desire for closeness and sexual contact can endure for a lifetime. It is often the constraints and restraints of social norms as depicted on television, in movies, and in bad jokes at the expense of older adults—by adult children and everywhere ageism is expressed—that scorn the idea of sexual activity among the elderly. Older adults do not define sexuality as penetrative intercourse alone but define the need and sensation of feeling loved as part of their sexual activity. This can be expressed in many ways: romantic words and activities, companionship, expressions of affection, stroking, and other forms of touch. In older men and women, interest in and desire for genital sex often shifts to a desire for intimacy. It is necessary for partners to speak openly about what it is that they wish, what they need to satisfy their needs for intimacy. Sometimes painful intercourse is the reason why sexual activity is avoided, and it may be caused by age-related thinning and dryness of vaginal tissue. This can be easily helped. If she is reluctant to talk about this, it is up to you to encourage her to talk to her doctor. Too often this topic is never discussed among this generation of people, who were raised to not discuss such matters. Time is running out! There's too much to be lost and not enough time to find what will bring pleasure to your lives.

FEARS, REASSURANCES, AND CAUTIONS

Terri, how do older people regard safe sex? We have heard that sexually transmitted diseases and HIV/AIDS are on the increase among the elderly. According to last year's White House AIDS and aging meeting, older age is not a safety net that protects people from getting HIV. New cases of HIV/AIDS are on the rise among the elderly. What contributes to this increase?

According to the Centers for Disease Control, many widowed and divorced people are dating again. They are not aware of their risks for HIV/AIDS and don't think they need to protect themselves. Women who no longer worry about becoming pregnant may be less likely to use a condom and to practice safe sex. Age-related thinning and dryness of vaginal tissue may raise older women's risk for HIV infection.

This can be helped if they will only go to their doctor and talk about it. I talk about drugs for erectile dysfunction. You know, when doctors prescribe Viagra they're usually not talking about condoms. Their whole purpose is to have penetrative sex with their partner, and we know that penetrative sex has many risk factors. Part of the reason is that medical providers are so uncomfortable talking about these things. They are often poorly informed themselves.

Some of the work that I've done is talking about a sexual model which gives patients permission to ask questions. They need to get information about sexual health using condoms and about not having penetrative sex.

We need to take a step back about erectile dysfunction. Their partner may not even know he is taking Viagra. The doctor just prescribes it when asked, without even exploring the relationship. The problem may not be with the erectile dysfunction but with the relationship, and Viagra is not going to solve the relationship. The drug may give them an erection, but that's not going to help the lack of communication in the relationship. It even may contribute to more resentment and anger because sex alone and not intimacy, the underlying issue, is not being addressed. We need to embrace our aging bodies, communicate about them, and understand them.

LGBTQ ISSUES

The possibility of same-sex marriage has lifted the burden of stress and anxiety that comes of denying the essence of a person's identity. You met **John M.** in chapter 2. John met his older, loving partner, Stuart, when he was in his early twenties and legal marriage was out of the question. When Stuart died suddenly at a still-youthful eighty, John, now the senior partner, met and could marry the much younger man to whom he is husband and mentor. It is a happy marriage that began with a beautiful wedding in the church they both love.

Terri, older men are increasingly coming out as gay or even transgender, sometimes after a lifetime of being straight. What are the consequences of this?

This issue is greatly affecting these men and their families. Their children are mourning the loss of their father. They have to reconnect with a parent of a completely different identity. There are parallel issues around loss and grieving as though there had been the death of a parent, issues such as, what does the future hold?

There are also serious issues about ageism in the gay community which affect men at this stage in their lives. In the gay culture there is a worship of male youth, male beauty, body image. There is a rift between younger and older gay men. Men who are coming out later in life have to bend to navigate that role of what it means to be gay. If you live in a large city, there are places to go. But where do you go if you live in the suburbs, exurbs, or rural areas? At this stage in their lives they are at a really isolating place. When gay men come out later in life they've lived their whole lives not being true to themselves. We live in a heteronormative culture. There are very strong messages that everyone is supposed to be heterosexual. You get married and you have a family or people wonder about you. When gay men were young, life was very difficult. You had to remain "in the closet" if you wanted to live life in the mainstream. Fortunately, attitudes about LGBTQ issues are changing quickly, particularly among the younger generations.

ONE TRANSGENDER MAN SPEAKS

I first knew **Sylvan O.** of Los Angeles, California, when he was a teenager and an exceptional young writer. He is still an exceptional writer, who is now a thirty-seven-year-old transgender man, having completed his transition at age thirty. It was wonderful to reconnect after twenty years.

I'm going to teach you a prefix now. The trans and queer community have created some new language to describe a person who is not trans. That prefix is from Latin, and it's cis. *Cis is the gender you were born with and conform to. Everyone, trans or cis, is aware that society imposes narratives about what a man or woman should be. And everyone has some relationship to those narratives. Even the introduction to your own book conveys that. What does it mean to man up? Who says you have to, and what does that mean?*

I can just say that every trans person has a different narrative about how they came to understand their own gender. Not every person has that "Maury Povich story" of "I'm a man trapped in a woman's body." That is not everyone's story. I never was a woman, what an average cis woman would think. I was always a man, but when I was younger the only way I could express the identity I felt was by identifying as a butch person, and I'm not even going to use the word lesbian, *because I don't like it.* Queer *and* butch *made sense to me because they conveyed masculinity. I'm not a man the way a cis man is acculturated or socialized to be a man. It's actually hard for me when cis or even queer women think of me, lump me in with all other cis men, because that has a history to me of domination. That's not who I am. It's a complicated nuance. I can only understand my own experience of being someone who doesn't fit in either of those man/woman boxes. I can't say I understand what it feels like to be a feminine woman or to be a man who is socialized as male. I can imagine.*

I think that the mark of a good writer is someone who can combine their imagination, experience, and research to create something that resonates with people. I think that a person who isn't trans could be really good or better at imagining someone different. Hopefully we are all doing our homework.

Was your family supportive?

I'm very fortunate to have very supportive parents. In my own lifetime, when I came out as gay, I think my mom was cool with it, but my dad struggled. When I came out as trans, I think my mom struggled a little. I don't know how much my dad struggled, but they got with the program quickly, and most of my family was totally supportive. They might have needed to do a little homework to understand. With the exception of one or two people, everyone in my family valued our family relationships so highly that no one would ever cast anyone out for such a reason.

And the rest of the world?

In terms of society at large, things are evolving. And I think part of my job as a young person is to be like "Come on, come on, faster, faster!" It's my job to agitate in that way, and I hope we keep doing that.

Stay tuned for Sylvan's observations of intergenerational relations in this age of the Longevity Revolution in chapter 9.

Sylvan observes his good fortune in having supportive parents. He is fortunate, also, in living in a time when, as difficult as facing being transgender is, awareness of the issue is light years ahead of where it was just a few decades ago. When **Jan Morris** (born James Humphrey Morris), a British journalist, historian, and travel writer, initially wrote about her transition in *Conundrum*,[6] first published in 1973, she caused a sensation. The change from James to Jan took place after having fathered five children and enduring doctors' warnings that great personality changes might result in the loss of the ability to write should she undergo the risky surgery. After fifty-eight years, as well as a legally required divorce after the sex change decades ago, Jan Morris and her wife are still together, and their marriage is civilly recognized again. Not only was Jan's talent unaltered, but she was recently voted the fifteenth-greatest British writer since World War II.

Public and published revelations by or about transgender individuals help clear the way for understanding and acceptance—and perhaps for the realization of what is at the heart of being human and beyond gender stereotyping or conforming to roles that don't fit everyone. Minds and hearts are expanded by *Transparent*, **Jill Soloway**'s successful and prize-winning Amazon television series, for example, about a family in which the father of adult children comes out as transgender, as did Jill's own father.

Among the growing number of writers whose own or whose family's experiences illuminate this issue are **Jennifer Finney Boylan**,[7] who tells her own story in *She's Not There: A Life in Two Genders*, among her many books and articles, and acclaimed journalist and author **Susan Faludi**,[8] who grew up with an authoritarian father, was separated from her father for twenty-five years, and reconciled eventually with the woman her father came out as.

AN AWAKENING FOR FATHERS

While the men we interviewed may not have volunteered information about their sex lives, several wanted to mention the change in attitude toward sexual orientation they themselves had undergone when they realized their children were gay. In particular, they spoke of feeling sympathetic and protective of gay daughters. Many spoke further about the changes in their attitudes about sexual orientation in general. You met **Walt Vail** in chapter 3. Here he is again:

> *When I was young, I was homophobic. I think I had trouble with gay men because when I was stationed in Lakehurst, near where I lived, for four months, I used to hitchhike and would invariably get picked up by men who would show me pornographic pictures or proposition me, and I'd tell them I was just looking for a ride. I had very negative feelings then, but my experience with my daughter and in the theater made me much more understanding.*
>
> *My wife was a great Girl Scout leader. Once she came home with our daughter, Gigi, from a campout with two other girls, the girls very giggly and acting secretive. My wife apparently knew what they were giggling about, was furious, and sent the others home. I was afraid my daughter would run away when I realized the situation. I consoled her and assured her that I knew many gay people from the theater who had happy lives and that I loved her no matter what. I know my wife was very upset. It was a surprise to both of us. I know that in high school my daughter spent a lot of time in her room, playing her ukulele, and I would go up and sit with her. She was lonely. I think there was one boy, who I believe was gay, who was her friend. She couldn't wait to get out of our very conventional town.*
>
> *When she married another woman, we danced together. She said, "Bet you never thought your little girl would get married." And I realized that somewhere in that little girl had been that dream.*

His wife's hostility toward their daughter's coming out as gay was a major factor in **David W.'s** divorce:

> *I found it hard to accept that my wife could cut her ties with our daughter. My wife had many gay—male—friends. While our son is divorced, our daughter is in a good marriage and has two wonderful children. Now that there are grandchildren, my ex-wife has had to eat crow to see them.*

KNOWLEDGE IS POWER

And ignorance is definitely not bliss, no matter how many people try to pretend it is. When you grew up, gender roles were clearly and rigidly defined, but human nature was no different then than it is today. Conforming to what was expected led to misery for many men and women, especially as they struggled through identity crises in adolescence. The United States was late among Western nations to accept the fact that Don't Ask, Don't Tell was a lose-lose policy, that sexual identity had nothing to do with bravery or loyalty to comrades in arms. Recognizing gender and sexual orientation differences, accepting them, and desensationalizing them is an ongoing process that has accelerated over the past two decades.

The hardened attitudes that led to hiding, shaming, and turning a blind eye yielded no good results in the last century. They led to repression and depression, as well as, all too often, to suicide. The move to a more open society doesn't change the numbers of people whose gender identity or sexual orientation is other than cis; it changes the acceptance of differences and recognition of our common humanity. The flare-ups of "moral indignation" and invitations to return to a social climate where "differences" were kept secret and individuals' reproductive and self-expressive rights were ignored lessen when our likenesses are valued more than our differences.

THE GOAL IS PLEASURE

Remember **Herbert G.** from chapter 2? In his healthy, vigorous nineties, he is a very social man, an appreciated companion, and a stimulating conversationalist.

When the cloud of depression since the loss of my beloved wife lifted, as my doctor said it would, I met a wonderful woman who was with other people I knew at dinner at a restaurant one night. Talking with her was so delightful we found ourselves continuing the conversation for a couple of hours together after the others had left. I woke up the next morning feeling wonderful. She had given me her phone number—she lived very nearby—and I called her and said, "Would you like another cup of coffee?" She laughed and said she would, but when I invited her to my place for it, she was highly insulted and let me know. I offered to come to her place or meet somewhere else. I finally understood that she had been deeply offended, thinking my invitation was a ploy to get her into my bed. It was kind of amusing to be thought of as a sexual predator when I never was, never could be, and it was far from my mind.

What was on his mind, Herbert told me, was what did develop: a close, intimate friendship. Shared season theater and concert subscriptions, shared confidences, caring about each other, deep affection. Herbert also helped educate me on the importance of touch—of a hug, holding a hand, or patting a shoulder in maintaining emotional well-being. He gave me a copy of the August 2015 issue of the Mayo Clinic's *Health Letter*, which was sitting on his desk and featured the article "Hold My Hand: The Power of Touch," evidence of his never-ending intellectual curiosity.

TERRI'S FINAL WORD

Terri Clark summed what she has learned and is teaching about sexuality and aging this way:

> *Sexual experience is positive as long as everyone involved takes proper precautions, consents, finds pleasure, and has a good time.*

8

SEPARATION, LOSS, MORTALITY, AND LEGACY

The Sense of an Ending

—Julian Barnes, book title

Of course it will happen. For some, it happens over and over again, not only in reality but also in anticipation or fear, replaying real traumas or rehearsing imagined catastrophes. For some, the fear becomes so overwhelming that they are surprised at their own ability to handle the reality when it finally happens. They are shocked that they're still standing. Fortunately, the perspective of age allows us to reflect on the many times loss has occurred in our lives and left us not only still standing but also stronger. It is paradoxical but true. This is one of the great gifts of time—especially unexpected longevity. From the first alarming separation from the womb (no wonder we cry!) to childhood losses of beloved toys, pets, friends, and adults in our lives, developing resilience prepares us for the separations experienced through family moves, new schools, new towns, new hurts, new jobs, new disappointments. Yet, as you reflect, you can say, as Maya Angelou famously said, "Still I rise."

ADVANTAGE: AGE

Most old painful memories are eventually lost, or at least fade, as we grow up and grow older. Some, without our realizing it, change us in ways we could not envision at the time: newly gained approaches to new situations and people, for example, or unconsciously adopted mannerisms of people we loved and admired. In time, once painful thoughts of those we lost make us smile instead of weep with the memory. Think back now to a time you thought a loss was impossible to survive. You did survive. So did the memory. The pain, if you still feel it, has lost its ability to pierce your heart as sharply. A shifting perspective is part of the healing.

The longer life span of today's man brings with it many more experiences of separation and loss. A sense of history helps to put it in perspective when we realize how abrupt our forebears' separations must have been when they left home, family, even country and culture without an Internet to bridge the divide. While the sense of separation is personally just as strong as men leave home, establish new roots, watch nests empty as children grow and leave, and seek new interests and work lives, the coping mechanisms at hand have changed in ways your fathers could not have imagined. In your own lifetime, you continue to experience the revolution in the ways we communicate. You are also among an increasingly rare group of men if you have stayed in one place of employment until retirement. Instead, you, like others you have met in these pages, have left jobs—or have had them leave you; even whole professions may have left you behind. You may have left youthful endeavors along the way as you've started new ones. You may be among the growing number of people over sixty who separate and divorce, as noted in chapter 6. Any of these may have had an accompanying wrench of separation—even, for some, much more than a wrench: a feeling of loss of identity.

Interestingly, these more frequent changes, marked along the way by both planned and unforeseen separations and inevitable losses, also yield compensating personal growth. Later challenges are met with the advantage of greater maturity. The reflective man looks back and realizes that he has not only survived but also gotten stronger. As physical strength may be lessening (or certainly feels different from his youth), his ability to use acquired mental, emotional, and moral strength to meet challenges is stronger than ever. His "bank" of self-knowledge and wisdom has been growing through deposits of experience, good and bad. The questions about dealing with loss in life may begin with *why* for philosophers. For most of us, the questions begin with not *why* but *when* they will happen and *what* they will be. Not *whether* (they happen) but *how* (we face them). No matter how prepared you are for loss, it's important to check in with your doctor and report its occurrence. Particularly for older people, grief can exacerbate existing medical conditions. Specific grief counseling from a licensed professional or professionally led bereavement groups is helpful to many. Those vainly seeking the "closure" that pop psychology and tabloids promote find that, as long we live and remember, closure is impossible and undesirable. We learn, eventually, to live with memories of those we lose as they remain part of us.

You met **Herbert G.** in chapter 2. He met his wife when she was fifteen and he was fifteen and a half. He told his parents that night that he had met the girl he was going to marry. Five years later she proposed "before we did anything wrong." They were married for seventy years. Loss began for both as her memory faded with Alzheimer's. On her last morning, Herbert had gone downstairs to buy her flowers and returned to find that she had slipped away finally and completely. He had been her primary caregiver for years leading up to that moment. When she was dying, his longtime, younger (Chinese) internist called him in for a sit-down and imparted what he described as his own "Chinese diagnosis." He told Herbert, "You're going to feel like you're in a dense, dark forest. One day a long time from now, you'll see a crack of light. Walk right into it. Make room for that path." Herbert found that to be true as he created an active older life full of new meaning while keeping treasured memories alive.

In chapter 5 you met **Mark S.**, an active, social person who actually described himself as "a basket case" following the loss of his wife and, later, his daughter. Recovery for Mark was not about "forgetting" or the unattainable process of "closure." Instead, he endured the grief, keeps his memories alive, and, as he put it, put his hand on the knob and opened the door. His life is full in ways he did not anticipate but allows himself to enjoy.

> *I've always been a positive thinker. I'm a glass-half-full person. That's what has helped me get through what I've gone through. I often ask myself how I survived losing a wife and a daughter in five years. Our family relationship has been unbelievably close. I don't know how I got through it. I take one day at a time. Oh, I have my moments. You can't lose two loves of your life without being gloomy. I have a drink every night; whether with people or alone, 5:30 is cocktail time— always was with my wife. Every night I toast my wife, and I toast my daughter. It's a ritual every single night.*

*Don't misunderstand me; nothing comes easy. I take one day at a time.
If I relax too much at home, I get very depressed, and I force myself to
do things. It doesn't come easy. When my daughter passed away I was
angry with God. I was so angry. I was turned off—to religion. It made
me question again, "How could He let the Holocaust happen? How
could You take my wife and my daughter in five years?" I still observe
religious holidays, though.*

Perhaps having survived the Battle of the Bulge as a double Purple
Heart veteran at a very young age helped shape Mark for the challenges
he has had to face. Rather than deny his grief and loss, Mark is fortunate
in being able to embrace his memories. Do you have ways of dealing with
gloom? Mark is very conscious of his own attitude toward living and
what he considers his good fortune in his temperament.

*I have a sister who's going to be ninety-eight, and she's the exact
opposite of me. One day I called and said, "Syl, where did this longevity come from?" And she said, "Who needed it?" One day she said to
me, "The doctor was here, and he had the nerve to tell me I'm going to
live to be over a hundred."*

The nerve? Clearly Syl does not see the doctor's prognosis as good news.

While the grief at the loss of a life partner is intense—and may be
crippling—the intensity is muted with time. The change in one's life is
permanent, but the experience of living continues, and the change is
eventually accompanied by growth. Much has been written about ways to
cope with such loss as well as the discovery of meaning and growth that
accompany the trauma. The work of Dr. Carolyn Walter and of Dr. Mark
Peterson, as both counselors and leaders in the field, is helpful in dealing
with loss on a practical and personal rather than a theoretical basis.[1]
Much has also been written about the importance of putting off important
decisions when loss is new. Remember **Leonard F.** in chapter 6? Waiting
and living through the experience of grief and its stages is tough but
important. Had he waited longer—and not eaten that casserole—no doubt
Len would have saved himself the trauma of a bitter second marriage, the
alienation of family and friends, and all kinds of upheaval in his life while
still learning that he had yet to work through the loss of his beloved
Sweetie, now further complicated by guilt and regret.

On the most practical levels, the bereaved are inundated with advice. Of course, everyone and every loss are different. All research and observations by grief counselors point to agreement that it is wise to avoid making hasty decisions, especially in matters as consequential as moving, for a year if possible. For some people who find staying in the same home impossible, even after several months, moving away temporarily makes returning later possible, although they realize that their grief accompanied them.

Without separations and losses, would it be possible to develop empathy? Their own life experiences and sense of empathy certainly feature in thoughts of legacy that follow.

LEGACY

We asked men if they thought about "legacy" in any sense—if they think about what happens after their lives. Some just said no. In other words, the ending is final. Not one who responded positively, however, did so in material terms, even if they have made plans to leave bequests to causes they care about or are already doing so. Not one—with the exception of Peter H., whom we met in chapter 5 and from whom we'll hear more below, talked about dividing property, however large or little, among survivors. The men you meet in this book run the financial gamut from very little to reasonably and very comfortable.

As we probed a bit, it was clear that some men we met view their legacy in terms of children or grandchildren. For instance, **Fred B.** of Atlanta, Georgia, who is raising two sons on his own, said,

> *A hundred years from now, it will not matter what my bank account was or the sort of house I lived in or the kind of car I drove. . . . But the world may be different because I was important in the life of a child.*

Jose S., whom we met in in chapter 3, thinks of "leaving a footprint" by participating in activities that matter:

> *I want to believe that the causes that I believe in will continue to impact society. I feel that my participation is part of continuing that work after I'm gone. I consider that part of legacy.*

Others had developing or already definite ideas. You may recall **Peter H.** from chapter 5. He is very involved with development projects in San Francisco.

Peter, do you ever think about what you're doing in terms of legacy?

I definitely would say yes. Not so much the Community Benefits District, because that's not creating something new. That's managing our neighborhood, making it a better place. The development projects, absolutely. One of the development projects in the Transbay area is developing an entirely new neighborhood of high-rise buildings from three hundred to five hundred feet, almost four thousand housing units. That's going to have a huge impact on this area. Because of the way it was set up, it's 30 or 35 percent affordable. As a matter of fact, I'm going to meet [my girlfriend] Susan in Paso Robles today, but I told her I've got to be back on Tuesday. I have to say my piece at the San Francisco Board of Supervisors to support a zoning change for a building we want to increase the height in, which will result in 60 percent affordable units.

So I would say, very much so. And the subway project. All this stuff would happen without me. They don't depend on me, but I'm helping to contribute. The lack of affordable housing out here is out of control. This project has gone on forever. We've just completed the first building down here—a thirty-story building. I've probably been doing this for twelve years on this citizen advisory committee and the developer selection panel with the old redevelopment agency. They're actually starting to lease out units down here. Whenever I walk down the street I see the building there.

There's another legacy thing . . . I hope I'll have enough money to last as long as I do. One never knows what is going to happen. I could walk out of here today and get run over by a minibus. And so I've got a fund set up at the University of Wisconsin through the university foundation for a small scholarship fund.

When I was in college, no one had to do anything. The tuition was about a hundred dollars a semester. We all had roommates, and I think I was paying about forty bucks a month for rent. I talked to the guy from the foundation. He said a lot of these kids today have to work. I asked him if I could set it up to have several different scholarships at five hundred dollars a month—if that would make a difference for these students. And so I thought, we make it for however much they could take out for three or four or five different scholarships every year for five hundred dollars a month. It will make a huge difference for some of these kids. I have it set up, and now I have to make sure I've dedicated some of my retirement funds to the university. Had I not gone to Madison, I would have had a completely different life. I was not a great student in high school at all. I was very rebellious. I didn't study. I didn't care about anything. I barely got in, and then I started doing well academically. It made all the difference for me. That's why I'm happy to do this.

For **Oliver Franklin**, whom you met earlier, in chapter 5, legacy is a definite preoccupation that has to do in part with history.

My son is nearing thirty and has a wonderful girlfriend. I want grand-children, but that's unfair. He was born when I was forty-one. I should have had him earlier if I wanted to make that argument. Legacy right now is about writing, leaving a record. I'm editing a book about Lincoln University and writing about my life at Oxford, for both of which I'm grateful. The saying is, "If you don't write it, it don't exist." Oral history—folklore—is gone or greatly distorted in two generations.

Mostly I think about legacy in terms of whether I moved the process forward. Did I ease somebody's pain? Did I make things better? Not whether people say I was a good man or a successful man. For five years I did a project at Girard College[2] with the Duke of York, sending black teenagers to England every summer. We had to overcome many obstacles to get the program started. But I'll never forget speaking at a charter high school's graduation in a church. The woman who introduced me had a master's degree from Penn State. To my surprise, she talked about having gone to England—in that very program—in her junior year of high school and how it changed her life. I was totally bowled over. She talked about what it was like to get out of her neighborhood, her city, her country and realize there was a wider world. That was good!

Charles D., whose story is told in chapter 4, had this to say about legacy:

> *What am I leaving to my kids, grandkids, wife? No wall in a hospital that will find my name on it. I can't just die, however. I have to have some sort of an ending, so it's okay to die. That's what I'm coping with right now. I've had four really close friends die. Close relationships, talking intimately, and not being able to share this with someone you care about and who cares about you—not able to go through this mutual experience together—is a real regret that I have. Sitting over vodka and talking about death and dying. How do you do it? You have to have these conversations while you're still capable of these conversations and come to some resolution so the children are okay with your leaving. That's my challenge for the future. One of my children wants to eulogize me while I'm alive because she doesn't want me to miss the things she will say about me. So I'm starting to think that maybe I should have a shiva in my lifetime.*

No decision about legacy for Charles yet, but it certainly sounds as though he's thinking about it. His daughter's wish to eulogize him now indicates we'd get a much different answer if we asked his children and grandchildren what they think his legacy will be. They would most likely have a great deal to say about the love, time, ideas, and experiences they shared with their father and grandfather, who was always interested in how they felt and what they thought—and let them know it.

Why no name on the hospital wall?

> *I do care about charity, and especially in my lifetime. I most admire people who give anonymously. I believe in the teaching of Maimonides [thirteenth-century rabbi and philosopher] about charitable giving. The highest form is to give someone a job and enable him to become independent. The next highest is giving anonymously. I'm a great admirer of Warren Buffet and Bill Gates and their determination to give their fortunes away. And the man who I believe inspires them, Charles Feeney, whose cover was blown years ago as the creator of a foundation [the Atlantic Philanthropies] that has given away his billions to causes that improve people's lives. I admire his avoidance of publicity, his values, and his modesty.*

WHEN LOSS SEEMS TO MAKE NO SENSE

Hardest to bear is loss out of order, the loss of a young person, even for those with a deep religious faith or strong spiritual sensibilities. Eventually, however, they find strength to place their loss in the context of the universality of the experience and to draw whatever meaning they can find from the life that was lost.

In the heart of the beautiful farmland of Pennsylvania Dutch country is the small city of Lancaster. There you will find a foundation called A Week Away, which is run by an unpaid, all-volunteer board and staff.[3] It was founded by **Caleb Walker**, son of Keith Walker, the pastor you met in chapter 1. Caleb was the third of the Walkers' four sons. His father says that if Caleb hadn't been ill, he would have played soccer for Penn State, like his next-oldest brother did. Instead of the playing fields, Caleb fought his battle in hospitals—against a rare form of cancer that attacks the brain and spine. Caleb faced his illness for five years and spent most of the last eight months of his twenty-four years of life building the foundation. Through brain surgeries, courses of radiation, and chemotherapy regimens, Caleb not only maintained his own strength of spirit but also recognized the effects of his illness on those around him, "his team."

Someone who felt Caleb could use some time away gave him and his best friend a weekend trip to Ocean City, New Jersey. Caleb remembered how that weekend was a time that made him feel like a normal person. He said that the time spent with his family, "combined with the peaceful ease of the trip," allowed him to dream of the possibility of one day living cancer-free. This was the inspiration for A Week Away, which hopes to give every immediate family member and/or primary caregiver "a week of peace in their chaotic world." Based on his own experience, Caleb felt that a week of peace together could enable them all to continue the fight.

PLANNING WHILE YOU ARE ABLE

Not long before his death, David Remnick interviewed Leonard Cohen, who said, "At a certain point, if you still have your marbles and are not faced with serious financial challenges, you have a chance to put your house in order. It's a cliché, but it's underestimated as an analgesic on all levels. Putting your house in order, if you can do it, is one of the most comforting activities, and the benefits of it are incalculable."[4]

One of the people who has most to teach us about how we can do this and came about his knowledge through a lifetime (more than seventy years) of personal experience, study, observation, and practice is **Mark Peterson**, EdD, of Philadelphia, Pennsylvania, and Freeport, Maine, whom we met in chapter 6. Mark realizes that he has always been creative and found satisfaction in working with his hands (woodworking) and in creating and starting programs. Not long after that first retirement, as we learned in chapter 6, he returned to work, busier than ever, with a new focus on how we make good decisions. We talked over coffee at the kitchen table:

> *Since my doctoral dissertation, I've been interested in how behavior is affected by emotions, really how cognition is influenced by emotion. Think, for example, how caring—emotion—which often is manifested in "not wanting to burden the children," leads to action in making preparation for end of life.*

Mark mentioned some reading that influenced and spurred his own thinking—Rushworth Kidder's *How Good People Make Tough Choices*, and a *New York Times Magazine* article, "What Broke My Father's Heart."[5]

> *I designed a class and started teaching at OLLI [Osher Lifelong Learning Institute at Temple University], the idea being to teach people how to prepare for the difficult decisions while they can. It started with a six-hour class; now it is ten hours, and people are asking for more.*
>
> *In my practice, and in the hospice work Carol and I both still do, I've had patients who "saw the light" and those who didn't. It makes me realize how much we don't know. Every single cell in our body screams for life. It's a visceral force. Some people struggle so hard against dying, while others say, "I'm ready." And we may not know how we'll feel, but we can know what we don't want. Personally, I know that I want better than 50 percent chance of survival before I agree to treatment.*

THE GIFT TO SURVIVORS

The choice for survivors or family is what to do or how to live with what-if when treatment is denied. Grief, while still present, is not the same as complicated grief. Complicated grief is accompanied by angst, depression, even guilt. Preparing for end of life is a great gift to survivors. We can relieve them of complicated grief.

Still, however, there's a great disparity between the numbers of people who care about end-of-life decisions and those who actually do something about them. For example, 80 percent of individuals want to die at home, but only about 20 percent do. Even more, 90 percent say that it is important to create medical directives for their health care and convey their wishes to their doctors. Without completing advanced medical directives it's possible to have your life and suffering extended far beyond what you would want. I want to make it possible for people to plan for the end of life while they are able and to involve and assist their families in the process. It benefits everyone.

Mark's ebook, *Your Life, Your Death, Your Choice*, provides all the tools necessary to create a legal document in order for those who care for and/or survive you to carry out your wishes. It is totally interactive and user-friendly, with links to videos, newscasts, podcasts, and articles. It provides suggestions and strategies for conversations with the person you designate as your medical proxy, your doctor, and those most important to you.

It's not surprising that Mark's classes have always been filled and students ask for more. We all have seen the difference between life endings that were good and not so good. Even though it may seem like a very uncomfortable thing to do, Mark has pinpointed where the stresses are and helps us recognize and overcome them.

This gift to survivors—and ourselves—is also part of legacy, knowing you have eased the burden of grief and set an example for those who are left.

DOES ALL THIS MEAN I'M MORTAL, TOO?

Running through all that Mark helps us do with and for our families and ourselves—and through the experience of loss, of caregiving, and of being cared for—and through recognizing the opportunities and challenges of the passage of time is the acceptance of our own mortality. Whether or not you believe in an afterlife, you still have the now to deal with and to live in. Recognizing mortality doesn't mean dwelling on it—especially if you let the thought get in the way of holding on to and making the most of living.

INSPIRATION IN LOSS

In retrospect, we remember being faced in the year 2000 with the devastating loss of Adele Magner, the fifty-eight-year-old founder of the Philadelphia Young Playwrights.[6] English professor, wife, and mother of a son and a daughter, Adele had founded a groundbreaking organization that fulfilled her vision of enabling students of all ages to find and express their voices through playwriting, providing teachers with the tools for their own development, and creating artistic teams of theater artists, teachers, and students working and learning collaboratively. She was able to bring together school districts and the theater community as well as a wide range of civic and corporate support. When Adele died after fifteen years of devotion to her dream and the realization of its success, her husband, **Alan Magner**, MD, of Yardley, Pennsylvania, and other family members found inspiration in Adele's life, work, and passion.

Alan, still a practicing physician, joined the Philadelphia Young Playwrights' board of trustees, and serving with him are Adele's son, Aron Magner (keyboardist of the jam band the Disco Biscuits), and her brother and sister-in-law. They have all been able not only to carry on Adele's legacy and see her vision grow but also to enrich their own lives as they continue a tradition of giving she started. The grandchildren she never knew are all still too young to help, but it is guaranteed they will know what their grandmother started and the values she passed on to inspire them to help others.

Sometimes a path through grief is in the memorialization of the person you lost. What did they care about? What was their passion? Most of us can never afford to build a memorial in concrete or stone, but we can memorialize the person through a volunteer effort or our own awakened interest in their behalf. The feeling in return is always positive. It is a healthy, positive way to direct your energy. Think of something you can do in honor of someone you lost.

9

WHO WILL YOU BE?

Our lives begin to end the day we become silent about the things that matter.

—Martin Luther King Jr.

We intended to call this chapter "Conclusions" until we realized, through all the interviews, the stories, the research, and so on, that there are no conclusions—and that is the best news of all. No endings, only openings. No closures, only absorbing and expanding. There are only new days and new possibilities, new horizons and new opportunities, and all require manning up (some more than others). We also realized that "manning up" is courage, as exemplified by men you met here. Being a new senior man has been influenced, it's true, by the advent of the new senior woman, the liberated one. Young men and women come closer to seeing each other as equals, as partners, as other human beings, while still saying, with the French, "Vive la différence!" and celebrating it. Giving up dominance is a relief, the relinquishing of an unnecessary and unwelcome burden in a world that sorely needs the best of all genders. And, of course, the new senior man still has the masculine advantage of being considered better looking and more interesting as he grows older. (So unfair.)

STILL THE SAME PERSON ... BUT

Yes, you are still the same boy inside, the one who was probably told to "man up." But you are so much more! You have layers and depths that boy could not foresee. Make a balance sheet. Consider the pivotal positive experiences of your life. Easy-peasy! Now consider the sum of the pivotal negatives, including losses. Remind yourself of how you emerged from the negative experiences, how you not only survived but eventually gained in strength, self-knowledge, empathy, and character. All of that is who you are now. Remember what Maya Angelou said? "Still I rise." That might be a good mantra to adopt should you need it. And you will. There will be challenging times again; you will be ready. You have the gift of time.

WHAT HAVE WE LEARNED?

The men in this book are all very different, of course; yet they share the qualities of resilience and openness to change. Most, we found, have a sense of humor that sharpens perspective and lets them realize that they are simultaneously the most important person in their own lives and as a grain of sand in the universe. They retain their independence even as they recognize and deepen family and friendship relationships and allow themselves to rely on others when necessary. For some, the end of traditional work life has led to satisfying new careers or interests or social lives. Some have learned to express feelings they quashed or left underdeveloped as they devoted themselves to striving for success or struggling to survive.

THE UPSIDES AND PROSPECTS OF "INTERESTING TIMES"

There is disagreement about whether "May you live interesting times!" is really an ancient Chinese curse or ought to be attributed to Confucius because it sounds like something he, in his wisdom, would have said. But we get it. And we are living in them, with the world spinning at an unanticipated, and sometimes terrifying, pace. On the upside, consider all the advantages your forebears never imagined that you live with every day—and take for granted: GPS, advances in medical research and care, flu shots at the drugstore, watching movies at home, Skype, all those Facebook friends, no more encyclopedia salesmen. All of the world's information is at your fingertips on the Internet—vicariously travel anywhere via your computer. The computer also makes possible starting a small service business from home or a blog of your own—or publishing an ebook. Whole worlds your grandfather never knew.

And you have twenty-four-hour news! Whoops. Should we really keep this in the "upside" column? (Surely there is a joke about how many pundits it takes to do something . . .)

Unless we choose not to, we now can know about everything that goes on in the world—the good, the bad, the ugly, the unsettling, the still-to-be-determined, and the not-verified or fake news. It is definitely part of what sometimes feels like chaos in these "interesting times." The upside lies in the fact that it is out of such times that new ideas and whole new ways of thinking emerge. Terrible and exciting at the same time. Opportunity abounds in how to help make these new ways positive.

Two of the men in this book are at near-opposite ends of the political spectrum; yet each devotes much of his postretirement time to the kind of activism that focuses on making their part of the world better. Each is taking the job we all have, the job of *citizen*, very seriously. You, as an activist for what you believe in, will always have work and be desperately needed if you are willing to do it. One request: Get out of the like-minded bubble, and talk to people on the other side as often as possible. Activism is not just what you do; it becomes a state of mind, one that involves you in something beyond and bigger than yourself. Frustration and depression yield to determination when you focus on something that can be done because you are helping. Definitely a win-win!

TIME TO MAN UP

By George, you've got it! Time! That's all you need. Like the men in this book, you've lived and learned, and still there is more time ahead. Time for new adventures, new learning, new inspirations; new strength of will and of character; new appreciation of what it means to be alive and part of the world. Instead of fearing or bemoaning the changes, you are manning up to be part of making them. You have time to do what Gil Stewart refers to as "growing into your gifts." Use the gift!

AFTERWORD

We began this book with every expectation that we would finish it together. Every bit of the planning, the outlining, the research, the interviewing, and much of the writing we were able to do together. Bobby Fleisher worked and lived, as she had for the past six years, with regular chemo treatments, borne always with gratitude for her doctors' vigilance and care, as well as her own indomitable strength, spirit, and resilience. If her sense of humor and optimism ever failed, it was never obvious to others. She continued to live the extraordinarily full life she always had, an active intellectual life filled with meaningful activities, like her ongoing work for the library at the Philadelphia Museum of Art and her Bayport community in Florida; her travel to and with her children and grandchildren in California, Massachusetts, and England; and her devotion to family and so many friends. She touched more lives than we can count and hoped to touch many more through this book, another way of seeing, encouraging, inspiring, and being inspired by men whose lives and culture have changed so dramatically over the past decades.

For Bobby, life was a force to be used to the fullest we are capable of using it. She did that to the end: being sure to mail her last vote to Florida and knitting for an as-yet-unconceived-but-hoped-for great-grandchild. Meeting and interviewing women for *The New Senior Woman* and men for this book were opportunities to explore life itself. Her belief in our shared humanity was steadfast, and our ability to tell our stories to each other enriches and expands our individual experiences in ways that are open to us all. That belief was rooted, perhaps, in Bobby's deep love of literature and immersion in the great-books discussions she shared with her husband, Dan, and many of their colleagues and friends over the years and in the places they lived in Philadelphia, Milwaukee, Berkeley, and Bayport.

Writing with another person makes for a special kind of intimacy and friendship. You literally are able to "finish each other's sentences." Finishing this book with what feels like half a brain has been daunting, and the patience and kindness of our editor, Suzanne Staszak-Silva, and of Rowman & Littlefield, our publisher, are much appreciated. The shared fun and laughter are missing, yet very strong in memory. But for the men in this book and for all who may read it, and for Bobby Fleisher, it has been a labor of love.

—Thelma Reese

Appendix I

DISCUSSION GUIDE

Many men belong to book discussion groups. Discussion groups about aging or retirement are found less frequently. They are growing in number, however, along with men's awareness of the benefits of sharing their experiences and stories. Men discover the value of their own experience and opinions as resources for others, as stimulants to their own thinking and involvement in the world, and in creating and strengthening social bonds. Friendships often result among members. We hope you have or will create a discussion group of your own. If no one volunteers to lead the group, just take turns sharing the responsibility of sending a reminder e-mail or call and leading the monthly or weekly or biweekly sixty- to ninety-minute discussion. Aim for an optimum group size of five to twenty members.

This book can be a springboard shared experience for your group. You might start first with asking the following: *As a consequence of reading this book, and this discussion, are there any changes you might now consider making in your life?* For each chapter, participants might discuss specific stories they found compelling.

Here are some topics you might consider at subsequent meetings:

- What does "manning up" mean to you? When did you first hear that expression? How did it make you feel then? Think of times in your life when you feel you rose to challenges that constituted "manning up" for you.

- What kind of planning have you done for this stage of your life? Have you prepared for financial needs? What else? Are you thinking about new interests or reviving old ones? What is meeting your emotional needs now?
- How are you engaging with the world? As a bystander or a participant? If you do participate, how and why? Do you think your participation matters? Can we discuss this topic without partisan anger and emotion clouding the discussion—and should/how can we do that?
- How is your life different from your father's? Your son's different from yours? What do you foresee for the next generation?
- What did you think about people your age when you were young? Has your thinking changed? How? What encourages you about people who are older than you? Do you have any role models? (Go beyond "yes" or "no" on this one; really talk about them.) Is ageism affecting you? How?
- Do you have end-of-life plans? Have you discussed them with those closest to you? Legacy thoughts?
- Have your ideas of fun changed over time? What do you find most entertaining now? Find something all of you in this group would enjoy doing together, and do it.
- How has technology affected your life? What do you use most; what would you miss most if it were suddenly gone? Do you think, on the whole, the Internet is a force for good or not? For this discussion, you might watch together *Lo and Behold, Reveries of the Connected World*, a documentary by Werner Herzog, available on Netflix. It will definitely stimulate discussion.
- Do you engage with people outside your own "bubble"? Other generations, other ethnicities? How do you make it happen?
- Have you traveled? What has travel meant in your life? Are you planning future travel? What, if anything, will be different about it?
- What have you learned lately? On your own? In classes? What talents and interests are you continuing to develop?
- Write a letter to your young self. Tell him some of the things you'd like him to know from this vantage point. Have a read-aloud.
- What are your attitudes toward your own children (or friends' children)—their lifestyles, partners, child-rearing practices, your place

in each other's lives? How do you express approval, disapproval, or concerns?

- If you are part of the sandwich generation—caught between adult children and aging parents—what do you see as your responsibility? How do you handle it?
- Have your attitudes toward possessions and material things changed? How about manners and morals?
- What gives the most meaning to your life now?
- Whether you are still working or not, do you volunteer? For what? What does that mean in your life?
- How are you managing your health and fitness?
- Pick a person you read about in this book. What does his story remind you of or make you think about?
- Have you ever taken part in a political movement or protest? What and when?
- What do role models mean to you? Are you conscious of being one yourself?
- What forks in the road are you glad you never took? How do you handle regrets?
- What is your action plan?

Appendix 2

RECOMMENDED ORGANIZATIONS AND RESOURCES

Your own community's houses of worship, libraries, museums, senior centers, hospitals, schools, and film festivals welcome volunteers.

You can Google any of the following nonprofit organizations by name, highlight the website, and find all the information you need for a life-changing opportunity.

- *AARP Foundation Experience Corps*: Places volunteers aged fifty and over in high-needs elementary schools across the country to help children who cannot read at grade level.
- *Boys & Girls Clubs of America*: Serve millions of young people, through membership and community outreach, at thousands of facilities. Find a local club and get involved.
- *Earthwatch Institute*: Provides opportunities to join scientists on field research and education trips around the world, with the aim of promoting understanding and action for a sustainable environment.
- *Elders Climate Action*: Go to http://www.eldersclimateaction.org to find out how to volunteer or to start a group where you live for this recently formed grassroots movement of elders who come together to influence climate-change policy.
- *Encore.org*: Advances the idea of leveraging the skills and talents of experienced adults to improve communities and the world, placing applicants with nonprofit organizations.

- *Global Volunteers*: Prepares individuals, groups, families, or couples to serve in life-giving community-development projects worldwide.
- *Habitat for Humanity*: Partners with people in your community, and all over the world, to help them build or improve a place they can call home. Habitat homeowners help build their homes alongside volunteers and pay an affordable mortgage.
- *Meals on Wheels*: Effectively improves health outcomes and quality of life for millions of clients each year. Volunteers help distribute prepared meals to seniors and other vulnerable populations.
- *Meetup*: A website that lets you search for and organize local events based on shared interests. Enables you to find a local meetup that interests you or plan your own meetup with others in your community.
- *OASIS Connections*: Offers courses geared toward older adults in more than fifty cities, including classes on the arts and humanities and technology use.
- *Peace Corps*: Provides opportunities around the world to make a change in every sense. Can even serve with your spouse or partner.
- *Road Scholar*: Arranges experiential learning experiences. More than five thousand learning adventures in one hundred fifty countries and all fifty states, serving more than one hundred thousand participants each year.
- *StoryCorps*: Is a national project instructing and inspiring people to record each other's stories. At Thanksgiving, StoryCorps encourages high school students to record conversations with a grandparent or an elder in their lives.
- *YMCA*: Offers programming and exercise classes for active older adults.
- *Your local school district*: Offer to tutor in reading or math at an elementary school near you.

NOTES

INTRODUCTION

1. Barbara Fleisher and Thelma Reese's blog is http://elderchicks.com.

2. Barbara M. Fleisher and Thelma Reese, *The New Senior Woman: Reinventing the Years Beyond Mid-Life* (Lanham, MD: Rowman & Littlefield, 2013).

3. Jennifer Harper, "'Dramatic' Increase: Plastic Surgery for Men Up by 43 Percent as They Compete in the Job Market," *Washington Times*, March 12, 2015, http://www.washingtontimes.com/news/2015/mar/12/plastic-surgery-43-percent-among-men-report/.

1. MANNING UP TO RETIREMENT

1. Becca Levy, PhD, is a professor of epidemiology and part of the Yale School of Public Health; see https://publichealth.yale.edu/people/becca_levy. profile.

2. Harry R. Moody, ed., "Why Don't We Get Rid of Aging?" *Human Values in Aging Newsletter*, December 1, 2016.

3. Michael S. Kimmel, *Manhood in America: A Cultural History*, 2nd ed. (London: Oxford University Press, 2005).

4. George E. Vaillant, *Aging Well: Surprising Guideposts to a Happier Life from the Landmark Harvard Study of Adult Development*, 1st ed. (New York: Little, Brown, 2003).

2. WHO AM I NOW THAT I'M RETIRED?

1. Transamerica Center of Retirement Studies, *Retirement Throughout the Ages: Expectations and Preparations of American Workers; 16th Annual Trans-america Retirement Survey of Workers* (N.p.: Transamerica Institute, 2015), https://www.transamericacenter.org/docs/default-source/resources/center-research/16th-annual/tcrs2015_sr_retirement_throughout_the_ages.pdf.

2. Jean Berko Gleason and Richard Ely, "Gender Differences in Language Development," in *Biology, Society, and Behavior: The Development of Sex Differences in Cognition*, ed. Ann V. McGillicuddy-De Lisi and Richard De Lisi (Greenwich, CT: Ablex, 2001), 133.

3. STAYING THE COURSE: LONGER, FARTHER, DEEPER

1. Michael Capuzzo, *The Murder Room* (New York: Gotham Press, 2010).

2. Alfred E. Stillman, *Home Visits: A Return to the Classical Role of the Physician* (Abingdon, UK: Radcliffe, 2007).

3. Alfred E. Stillman, "Modern Times," *New England Journal of Medicine* 333 (October 19, 1995): 1086–87.

4. NEW PATHS

1. Vic Compher [John Victor Compher], *Lebensstrom Gedichte = Life-stream* (Goldebek, Germany: Mohland Verlag, 2008).

2. John Victor Compher, *Family-Centered Practice: The Interactional Dance beyond the Family System* (New York: Human Sciences Press, 1989).

3. Visit http://www.theartwell.org, http://www.interfaithcenterpa.org, and http://www.interfaithpeacewalk.org, respectively.

5. MEANDERING

1. The Best Day of My Life So Far, http://www.thebestdayofmylife.org.

2. The senior center that Roland frequents is Center in the Park (http://www.centerinthepark.org).

3. William Thomas, *Second Wind: Navigating the Passage to a Slower, Deeper and More Connected Life* (New York: Simon and Schuster, 2014).

4. Annie Levy, "Finding His Inner Artist," *Neurology Now* 11, no. 4 (August/September 2015): 38, http://journals.lww.com/neurologynow/Fulltext/2015/11040/Finding_His_Inner_Artist__For_John_Creveling_67,.25.aspx.

5. John P. Creveling, "The Wall," from his forthcoming book *I'm More Than What You See* (2017).

6. MY LIFE AT HOME FEELS DIFFERENT

1. Howard S. Friedman and Leslie R. Martin, *The Longevity Project: Surprising Discoveries for Health and Long Life from the Landmark Eight-Decade Study* (New York: Hudson Street Press, 2011).

2. Many of these statistics can be found in the US Census Bureau publications *Centenarians: 2010* and "The Older Population: 2010" (census brief from the 2010 Census), as well as elsewhere on the Census Bureau website. Newspaper articles that cite the Current Population Survey data include Tim Henderson's "More Americans Living Alone, Census Says," *Washington Post*, September 28, 2014, and Rachel Swarns's "More Americans Rejecting Marriage in 50s and Beyond," *New York Times*, March 1, 2012.

3. Richard Fry, "More Millennials Living with Family Despite Improved Job Market," Pew Research Center, July 29, 2015, http://www.pewsocialtrends.org/2015/07/29/more-millennials-living-with-family-despite-improved-job-market/.

4. Dhruv Khullar, "How Social Isolation Is Killing Us," *New York Times*, December 22, 2016, http://www.nytimes.com/2016/12/22/upshot/how-social-isolation-is-killing-us.html.

5. Leland Kim, "Loneliness Linked to Serious Health Problems and Death Among Elderly," UCSF News Center, June 18, 2012, http://www.ucsf.edu/news/2012/06/12184/loneliness-linked-serious-health-problems-and-death-among-elderly.

6. AARP Livable Communities, "The United States of Aging Survey—2012," AARP.org, September 5, 2012, http://www.aarp.org/content/dam/aarp/livable-communities/old-learn/research/the-united-states-of-aging-survey-2012-aarp.pdf.

7. Visit Friends in the City's website at http://www.friendscentercity.org.

8. Richard M. Gollin, *A Viewer's Guide to Film: Arts, Artifices, and Issues* (New York: McGraw-Hill, 1992).

9. At St. John's, as at many senior communities, short-term rental policies make it possible to try out new living arrangements before committing to long-term or permanent changes.

10. US Department of Health and Human Services, "Find Your Path Forward," https://longtermcare.acl.gov/the-basics/.

7. HEALTH, SEX, AND INTIMACY

1. Katie Hafner, "Researchers Confront an Epidemic of Loneliness," *New York Times*, September 5, 2016, https://www.nytimes.com/2016/09/06/health/lonliness-aging-health-effects.html.

2. To search for mental-health-care assistance, visit the Anxiety and Depression Association of America's website at https://www.adaa.org/finding-help.

3. American Cancer Society, "Key Statistics for Prostate Cancer," January 5, 2017, https://www.cancer.org/cancer/prostate-cancer/about/key-statistics.html.

4. Perry Epler Gresham, *With Wings as Eagles* (Winter Park, FL: Anna Publishing, 1980). Also, in this quotation, all emphasis is original.

5. Visit Action Wellness online at https://www.actionwellness.org.

6. Jan Morris, *Conundrum* (London: Faber, 1973).

7. Jennifer Finney Boylan, *She's Not There: A Life in Two Genders* (New York: Crown/Archetype, 2004).

8. Susan Faludi, *In the Darkroom* (New York: HarperCollins, 2016).

8. SEPARATION, LOSS, MORTALITY, AND LEGACY

1. See Carolyn Ambler Walter, *The Loss of a Life Partner: Narratives of the Bereaved* (New York: Columbia University Press, 2003), and Mark B. Peterson, *Your Life, Your Death, Your Choice: How to Have Your Voice to the End of Your Life* (Minneapolis: PublishGreen, 2016).

2. Girard College is a full-scholarship boarding school for academically capable students from qualified families of limited financial resources. It was originally founded almost two hundred years ago for "poor, fatherless white boys." Today's students are boys and girls of racially and ethnically diverse backgrounds.

3. Visit A Week Away's website at http://www.aweekaway.org.

4. David Remnick, "Leonard Cohen Makes It Darker," *New Yorker*, October 17, 2016, http://www.newyorker.com/magazine/2016/10/17/leonard-cohen-makes-it-darker.

5. Rushworth M. Kidder, *How Good People Make Tough Choices* (New York: HarperCollins, 2003), and Katy Butler, "What Broke My Father's Heart,"

New York Times Magazine, June 18, 2010, http://www.nytimes.com/2010/06/20/ magazine/20pacemaker-t.html.

    6. Visit the Philadelphia Young Playwrights online at http://www. phillyyoungplaywrights.org.

BIBLIOGRAPHY

AARP Livable Communities. "The United States of Aging Survey—2012." AARP.org. September 5, 2012. http://www.aarp.org/content/dam/aarp/livable-communities/old-learn/research/the-united-states-of-aging-survey-2012-aarp.pdf.

American Cancer Society. "Key Statistics for Prostate Cancer." American Cancer Society. January 5, 2017. https://www.cancer.org/cancer/prostate-cancer/about/key-statistics.html.

Boylan, Jennifer Finney. *She's Not There: A Life in Two Genders*. New York: Crown/Archetype Press, 2004.

Butler, Katy. "What Broke My Father's Heart." *New York Times Magazine*, June 18, 2010. http://www.nytimes.com/2010/06/20/magazine/20pacemaker-t.html.

Capuzzo, Michael. *The Murder Room*. New York: Gotham Press, 2010.

Compher, John Victor. *Family-Centered Practice: The Interactional Dance beyond the Family System*. New York: Human Sciences Press, 1989.

——— [Vic Comphor, pseud.]. *Lebensstrom Gedichte = Lifestream*. Goldebek, Germany: Mohland Verlag, 2008.

Faludi, Susan. *In the Darkroom*. New York: HarperCollins, 2016.

Fleisher, Barbara M., and Thelma Reese. *The New Senior Woman: Reinventing the Years Beyond Mid-Life*. Lanham, MD: Rowman & Littlefield, 2013.

Friedman, Howard S., and Leslie R. Martin. *The Longevity Project: Surprising Discoveries for Health and Long Life from the Landmark Eight-Decade Study*. New York: Hudson Street Press, 2011.

Fry, Richard. "More Millennials Living with Family Despite Improved Job Market." Pew Research Center. July 29, 2015. http://www.pewsocialtrends.org/2015/07/29/more-millennials-living-with-family-despite-improved-job-market/.

Gleason, Jean Berko, and Richard Ely. "Gender Differences in Language Development." In *Biology, Society, and Behavior: The Development of Sex Differences in Cognition*, edited by Ann V. McGillicuddy-De Lisi and Richard De Lisi, 127–54. Greenwich, CT: Ablex, 2001.

Gollin, Richard M. *A Viewer's Guide to Film: Arts, Artifices, and Issues*. New York: McGraw-Hill, 1992.

Gresham, Perry Epler. *With Wings as Eagles*. Winter Park, FL: Anna Publishing, 1980.

Hafner, Katie. "Researchers Confront an Epidemic of Loneliness." *New York Times*, September 5, 2016. https://www.nytimes.com/2016/09/06/health/lonliness-aging-health-effects.html.

Harper, Jennifer. "'Dramatic' Increase: Plastic Surgery for Men Up by 43 Percent as They Compete in the Job Market." *Washington Times*, March 12, 2015. http://www.washingtontimes.com/news/2015/mar/12/plastic-surgery-43-percent-among-men-report/.

Henderson, Tim. "More Americans Living Alone, Census Says." *Washington Post*, September 28, 2014.

Khullar, Dhruv. "How Social Isolation Is Killing Us." *New York Times*, December 22, 2016. https://www.nytimes.com/2016/12/22/upshot/how-social-isolation-is-killing-us.html.

Kidder, Rushworth M. *How Good People Make Tough Choices*. New York: HarperCollins, 2003.

Kim, Leland. "Loneliness Linked to Serious Health Problems and Death Among Elderly." UCSF News Center, June 18, 2012. http://www.ucsf.edu/news/2012/06/12184/loneliness-linked-serious-health-problems-and-death-among-elderly.

Kimmel, Michael S. *Manhood in America: A Cultural History*. 2nd ed. London: Oxford University Press, 2005.

Levy, Annie. "Finding His Inner Artist." *Neurology Now* 11, no. 4 (August/September 2015): 38. http://journals.lww.com/neurologynow/Fulltext/2015/11040/Finding_His_Inner_Artist_For_John_Creveling_67,.25.aspx.

Maroon, Joseph. "Late-Life Renewal Can Reward Those Who Do 'Right Thing' at the Right Time." *Pittsburgh Tribune-Review*, June 27, 2016. http://triblive.com/news/healthnow/perspectives/10681626-74/renewal-aging-perspectives.

Moody, Harry R., ed. "Why Don't We Get Rid of Aging?" *Human Values in Aging Newsletter*, December 1, 2016.

Morris, Jan. *Conundrum*. London: Faber, 1973.

Novotney, Amy. "The Real Secrets to a Longer Life." *Monitor on Psychology* 42, no. 11 (December 2011): 36. http://www.apa.org/monitor/2011/12/longer-life.aspx.

Peterson, Mark B. *Your Life, Your Death, Your Choice: How to Have Your Voice to the End of Your Life*. Minneapolis: PublishGreen, 2016.

Remnick, David. "Leonard Cohen Makes It Darker." *New Yorker*, October 17, 2016. http://www.newyorker.com/magazine/2016/10/17/leonard-cohen-makes-it-darker.

Transamerica Center of Retirement Studies. *Retirement Throughout the Ages: Expectations and Preparations of American Workers; 16th Annual Transamerica Retirement Survey of Workers*. N.p.: Transamerica Institute, 2015. https://www.transamericacenter.org/docs/default-source/resources/center-research/16th-annual/tcrs2015_sr_retirement_throughout_the_ages.pdf.

Stewart, Gil. *The Tanner Chronicles*. 11 vols. Aumsville, OR: October Years Press, 2012–2016.

Stillman, Alfred E. *Home Visits: A Return to the Classical Role of the Physician*. Abingdon, UK: Radcliffe, 2007.

———. "Modern Times." *New England Journal of Medicine* 333 (October 19, 1995): 1086–87.

Swarns, Rachel L. "More Americans Rejecting Marriage in 50s and Beyond." *New York Times*, March 1, 2012.

Thomas, William. *Second Wind: Navigating the Passage to a Slower, Deeper and More Connected Life*. New York: Simon and Schuster, 2014.

US Department of Health and Human Services. "Find Your Path Forward." LongTermCare.gov. https://longtermcare.acl.gov/the-basics/.

Vaillant, George E. *Aging Well: Surprising Guideposts to a Happier Life from the Landmark Harvard Study of Adult Development*. 1st ed. New York: Little, Brown, 2003.

Walter, Carolyn Ambler. *The Loss of a Life Partner: Narratives of the Bereaved*. New York: Columbia University Press, 2003.

ABOUT THE AUTHORS

Thelma Reese, EdD, retired professor of English and education, taught at Temple University, Arcadia University, and the Community College of Philadelphia. She created the advisory council for Hooked on Phonics and was its spokesperson in the 1990s. In that role, and as director of the Mayor's Commission on Literacy for the City of Philadelphia, she appeared frequently on television and hosted a cable show in Philadelphia. She also organized the Family Literacy Symposium at UNESCO in Paris in the 1990s. With Barbara Fleisher, coauthor of *The New Senior Woman*, Reese created and maintains the popular blog, http://www.elderchicks. com. Dr. Reese, a lifelong Philadelphian, is a wife, mother, and grandmother.

Barbara M. Fleisher, BA, MA, EdD (1931–2016), was a graduate of the University of Pennsylvania and the University of San Francisco and a retired professor of education. She wore many hats in her life: public school teacher; learning-disabilities and reading specialist; child advocate; college professor in San Francisco, Milwaukee, and Philadelphia; author; and—most important—wife, mother, grandmother, and great-grandmother. She authored many articles that have appeared in juried journals and presented her research at national and international conferences on reading. She was project director of several university-community partnership grants. With her coauthor, Thelma Reese, she created the blog http://www.elderchicks.com as the two embarked on writing their first book, *The New Senior Woman: Reinventing the Years Beyond Mid-Life* (2013).

NOV 0 8 2017